For Goose & Teddy,

The world we make is the future you inherit.

PROFESSIONAL ENDORSEMENT

Captain Barry Schiff – Award winning journalist and author with over 28,000 flying hours in 363 different aircraft. He first obtained his CFI in 1956, and he has written 13 books. He is a contributing editor at Aircraft Owners and Pilots Association:

Blue Water Ditching is an excellent treatise about a critically important subject, an excellent insurance policy against disaster. I pray that I will never need to use the life-saving principles you explain so well. Your book is a survival tool belonging in every pilot's library.
Best, Barry"

Colonel Robert "Dirt" Winston is a retired United States Air Force Command Pilot with 4,000 flying hours, mainly in C-130 Combat Transport and HC-130 Combat Rescue aircraft.

Every time that I flew across the "Pond" while reroute to Europe, the Middle East, or to South America I would look down at the vast ocean below and say a silent prayer that I wouldn't have to ditch. That silent prayer was the only hope I had, because I knew that I was not properly prepared for ditching. The training that I'd received in the Air Force was very thorough about how to survive once you were in a raft, but when it came to the subject of ditching, I was only advised to try to land on the swell and that most likely I would be killed in the impact. Dave's Blue Water Ditching is the answer to that silent prayer. This second edition must be in everyone's library. Dave offers water landing techniques that go much deeper than, "try to land on the swell." Dave logically leads readers through preparations before going "feet wet." All aspects of communications are discussed. Dave even offers a pre-ditching checklist. Blue Water Ditching will prepare pilots to successfully survive a ditching and save lives while doing so. I have had the honor of flying with Dave on many demanding missions and he was always the pilot that I wanted to fly with in combat. If I am ever in a ditching situation, I want Dave at the controls!

DEDICATION

This book is dedicated to the engineers who design, production experts who assemble and maintainers who maintain…the greatest machines mankind has ever built.

It is their efforts which have allowed the operators to fly the millions of flight hours of the last century. Without these men and women, I and my fellow operators would be driving trucks, trains and boats.

ABOUT THE AUTHOR

Major Dave Montgomery is a retired United States Air Force Command Pilot. He holds both a Federal Aviation Administration Airline Transport License with type ratings in the CE680, EMB-505, C-130, B-727, B-707, C-212, G-III, and G-IV and single engine land and sea privileges as well as FAA Certified Flight Instructor. He is currently flying as a Captain in the Cessna Latitude. He has accumulated 16,500 flight hours and has transited 76+ countries. His career experiences leave him well suited in this research project. He began this project in November 2008. Edition 2 was written in 2024.

OFFSHORE LANDING EXPERIENCE: In 1991, then Captain Montgomery was one of three special operations pilots to conduct an operational test and evaluation of the Lake Seawolf amphibious aircraft which included off-shore operations in the Atlantic Ocean. He writes about takeoffs and landings on parallel swells and on mixed sea chop from experience, something very few pilots can do.

SEARCH AND RESCUE EXPERIENCE: While on active duty in 1995 to 1998 he served as Air Force Liaison to the Civil Air Patrol as advisor for the search and rescue mission. In that capacity he was exposed to daily training and operations of the Search and Rescue community.

OCEANIC CROSSING CURIOSITY/EXPERIENCE: In 1982 while sitting in the right seat of a C-130 he looked down at the Atlantic Ocean while crossing 30° west…and said to himself, "dang if you land out here, who is going to come get you?"

Years later after logging 70+ oceanic crossings he began research as to what happens in a ditching scenario when a very ordinary day crossing went drastically awry. It was August 2004 and then Major Montgomery was the aircraft commander of a USAF Gulfstream while crossing the North Atlantic with a crew of five and six passengers. At 40,000 feet the main door seal failed and the aircraft rapidly decompressed. The experience (and successful outcome) sparked his interest in all the things that he did not know about oceanic flights and emergencies.

Miles, Claire and Dave in 2011

(THEY ARE NOW IN COLLEGE)

EDITION 2

After ten years on the speaking tour and talking with hundreds of crew members I want to share questions and answers from the field.

Second, I relay to the reader what is happening in the Search and Rescue World around the world.

I remind everyone that in the 1960s, 70s, 80s, and 90s we trained ditching because it happened. The risk was big.

Today the risk is much smaller as we use engines that seemingly never quit, fuel tanks that do not leak, electrical and pressurization grids which maintain their integrity and interiors that will not burn due to flame retardant materials. Modern aircraft have on-board systems to avoid severe weather and these systems improve yearly.

So, what is our threat? Hail, volcanic ash, fuel loss, uncontrollable fire, uncontained engine failure, a bad actor…

CONTENTS

+Indicates new information in Second Edition

LESSONS

On July 19, 1989 United Airlines Flight 232, a DC-10, was enroute from Denver to Chicago when failure of the center engine ruptured all hydraulic lines and the crew lost all hydraulic systems on an aircraft that relied on hydraulic fluid to move the flight controls. The three officers on the flight deck under direction of Captain Al Haynes (plus another pilot who was on board as a passenger), used a technique described as split throttle control to bank the airframe left and right, and descend the airframe in a semi-controllable fashion for the crash landing in Sioux City, Iowa.[1] 184 souls survived.

Flash forward to November 22, 2003 as a DHL A-300 departs Bagdad flown by Captain Eric Gennotte and First Officer Steeve Michielsen and is struck by a missile. The left wing was afire as the jet lost all hydraulic pressure. Captain Gennotte had attended a safety seminar earlier in the year[2] in which Captain Al Haynes was the guest speaker lecturing about split throttle technique and combatting the phugoid oscillations that occur during the maneuvering. With all flight controls knocked out on the Airbus, the crew used Captain Haynes' teachings and returned to the airport. The crew lived.

It is a fascinating read of airmanship, knowledge transfer and luck.[3] After cheating death x1,000 the aircraft landed and rolled into a minefield!

---

[1] http://clear-prop.org/aviation/haynes.html

[2] http://www.spacedaily.com/news/iraq-03a.html

[3] http://www.flightglobal.com/news/articles/great+escape-191713/

We all have lessons to learn.

No one is too experienced or too old to learn a new lesson.

INTRODUCTION

Professional air crews today have doctorate levels of aviation knowledge. It is my goal to bring ocean crossing crews up to that same level in the specialized field of ditching preparation and survival. Pilots are well aware each and every aspect of flying are never covered in one study book. Pilots are expected (and in most cases required) to know: the how and why aircraft can fly (aerodynamics); the how this particular aircraft can fly (aircraft operations manual); the how we are regulated (Federal Aviation Regulations); rules of the road (Airman Information Manual); and company operating procedures (Flight Operations Manual) and this list goes ON AND ON.

International operations add chapters regarding ICAO differences, customs, communication procedures, entry requirements, and agriculture requirements. ETOPS adds huge amounts of information on aircrew and airframe certification, diversions, emergencies, long range communications, and weather implications.

This guide provides a single source document which places the pertinent data about ditching into the hands of the crew member.

All ocean crossing aircrews face the chance of a blue water ditching. Thankfully the risk is low and instances are very few and very far between. The chances of this disaster are tremendously decreased thanks to 70+ years of modern engineering and advanced manufacturing processes which produce today's extraordinary aircraft. Among those accomplishments are engines that seemingly never fail, fuel tanks that don't leak, fuselages that maintain integrity after multiple thousands of expansions and contractions during pressurization while enduring extreme temperature swings, electrical systems which don't short out and cause fires, fire resistant interiors that don't ignite easily, and excellent fire extinguisher detection and suppression systems for complex engines and some baggage holds. Today's airframes are truly marvels of engineering and manufacturing which have accomplished remarkable safety records while amassing millions of flight hours.

The safe operation of modern aircraft encompasses many lines of defense in order to maintain the very impressive safety records. The first line is very meticulous and detailed engineering. Second comes the support mechanisms that are responsible for writing the 'how to' manuals, making the drawings, building the books and guides for the suppliers, maintainers and operators. Next the many vendors and contractors begin providing parts and pieces to make the sub-systems come together as an airframe. After days or weeks on the assembly line, the complete airframe rolls out the hanger door and is met by the flight line test crew who ensures all the sub-systems, parts and pieces operate as advertised. Next the test or acceptance crews take the airframe airborne to prove the 'standards' have been met and the airframe is ready for delivery.

During the operations life of the airframe, parts suppliers, maintainers, inspectors and analyst track the myriads of phase inspections, time inspections, cycle inspections, mandated inspections, airworthiness directives, and crew write ups to keep the airframe 'safe' (and making money).

At the USAF Advance Instrument Flying Course in San Antonio[4], there is a large plank hanging above the speaker's lectern: "The Aircrew Is A Defense Against An Accident – But It Must Never Be The Last Line Of Defense". But I promise you today, the aircrew <u>is</u> the group called on when airborne disaster arises. There are many people and computers on the ground that can offer advice and help…but they can never land your aircraft. No one can do it for you. Remember the Boy Scout motto: BE PREPARED.

A well trained crew is the last line of defense, in keeping the airframe airborne and bringing it down safely when everything goes from warm and safe to the state of mayhem which can come from the myriad of possible emergencies.

I emphasize last line of defense by highlighting these two recent extreme emergencies which were never dreamed of and certainly never trained for. These examples in recent history exemplify crews who were not trained in a specific event, but they overcame huge hurdles to achieve a successful outcome. These highly publicized examples of aircrews grasping success from the jaws of disaster have occurred in the last 25 years.

---

[4] Recently moved to OKC

In 1989 United Airlines Flight 232, a three engine DC-10, suffered a #2 engine uncontained failure which ruptured and destroyed all three hydraulic systems crippling the aircraft flight control systems.[5] The highly experienced crew was faced with multiple failures which they were not trained for. They did a remarkable job of controlling and crash landing the aircraft using the technique of 'splitting the throttles' to control pitch, roll, and speed which saved lives as they demonstrated superior airmanship over incredible odds.

In 2009, as US Airways flight, Cactus 1549, an Airbus twin engine A-320, suffered massive geese strikes and lost both engines while departing La Guardia, NY. The crew performed a water landing on the Hudson River saving all onboard. A second superb example of superior airmanship overcoming incredible odds.[6]

---

[5]http://www.airdisaster.com/cgi-bin/view_details.cgi?date=07191989&reg=N1819U&airline=United+Airlines

[6]http://www.airdisaster.com/cgi-bin/view_details.cgi?date=01152009&reg=N106US&airline=US+Airways

It is a safe bet to predict that there will be a blue water ditching by an airliner, freighter or large corporate aircraft in the future. Fate (known as bad luck or indeterminate outcome) and mother nature (which I define in aviation terms as weather, human error and gravity) have conspired against the aviation industry since inception and there is no reason to think all future ocean crossing aircrews are immune from disaster.

North Atlantic airspace is the busiest oceanic airspace in the world with about 1,300 flights a day,[7] most of which are large commercial carriers. 1,300 times 365 is 474,500 per year.

The Pacific area of operations logs some 625 flight a day[8] coming or going from North America. 228,000 per year.

Edmonton Air Control Center handles 38 polar crossing flights per day[9]. 13,800 per year.

---

[7] http://en.wikipedia.org/wiki/Gander_Automated_Air_Traffic_System

[8] FAA Western Pacific Communications Team; 1/11/2011

[9] http://www.faa.gov/about/office_org/headquarters_offices/ato/service_units/enroute/oceanic/cross_polar/ See CPWG1 Nav Canada Update

So, the North Atlantic, North Pacific, and Polar Regions combine for some 716,300 flights a year to/from/across the North American continent. That is on average 1,962 every day. Add in to the statistics the number of flights over the South Atlantic, South Pacific, Indian Ocean, Southern Ocean, Arctic Ocean, and all of the seas and gulfs and the thousands of inter-island flights that face a ditching possibility, and we can conservatively estimate there are over a million blue water flights a year. That is 2,700+ flights a day. If Las Vegas or Ladbrokes were to make book on the statistic, what would the odds be?

Search and rescue forces around the world are certainly aware of these risks. Recently a first mass rescue drill was held with a scenario of a large passenger aircraft polar ditching. The tabletop exercise involved Reykjavic OACC, ARCC Sondestrom, and SAR Norway. Other exercises are planned.[10]

[10] FAA Cross Polar Working Group (CPWG) CPWG/8-IP/10; 02/12/2009

Fate and Mother Nature Versus Engineers and Production Experts

At the time of this writing, news of the week November 4 - 10, 2010 is a perfect example of how Fate and Mother Nature continue in their conspiracy against aviation, advanced engineering, and aircraft manufacturers. I do not want to guess what outcomes will result from the incidents of that week. My intent is only to point out the headlines. The cause of these incidents is NOT what is important. I use the occurrence of these three events to beautifully illustrate my point.

First, the newest product of Airbus is the four engine A-380. On November 4, 2010 one of the aircraft (there were about 26 flying that week) experienced an uncontained engine failure.[11] This is one of the newest, greatest, most technologically advanced, and largest (466 souls onboard) airframes in the world. This uncontained failure should not have happened. An engine failure is understandable. It occasionally can happen. But an uncontained failure…that allowed engine parts to explode and puncture fuel tanks and knock out hydraulic and electrical systems and damage the wing? That is NOT supposed to happen, but it did. Thankfully the crew recovered the aircraft with no injuries, except to the egos and reputations of the Rolls Royce and Airbus engineers.

---

[11] Wall Street Journal; Saturday November 6, 2010, page A9

My second example of the Fate and Mother Nature conspiracy occurred on November 9, 2010 as one of the flying test bed twin engine Boeing 787s (there were approximately four flying that week) had to make an emergency landing in Laredo, Texas due to smoke and/or fire in the back of the jet[12] caused by some electrical problem. After landing the crew used slides to exit the aircraft. Pilots know that a ground egress using slides is serious. It generally indicates the crew was in quite a hurry to vacate the airframe due to the smoke or heat or both.

The third example of the conspiracy occurred on November 8, 2010 as the 952 feet long luxury liner Carnival Splendor with 4,446 people onboard was 200 miles south of San Diego when a fire erupted in the engine room cutting off power, phones, air conditioning, and most importantly, crippled the ship so could not move under it's own power and had to be towed to port[13]. The ship was only <u>two years old</u>.

The cause or outcome or fix of these events is not pertinent to my point. My point is the best engineers in the world at Airbus (France), Boeing (USA), and Fincantieri Ship Company (Italy) can design, and the most talented production folks in the world can build the most remarkable machines mankind has ever seen, and a kinked electrical wire, or a twisted pneumatic line, or a wrong sized oil tube, or an in-correctly torqued nut, or a loose fuel line, or a poorly designed fuel control unit, or a piece of loose insulation or FATE AND MOTHER NATURE can still wreak havoc on the designers, builders and operators who command these machines.

---

12 Wall Street Journal; Wednesday November 10, 2010, page B1

13 Wall Street Journal; Wednesday November 10, 2010, page A6

Professional training centers at the major airlines and corporate training centers offer some sort of swimming pool introduction to water survival. Aircrew members from the newest beginner to the most experienced study and review how to brief and prepare passengers on (1) how to exit a fuselage, (2) how to inflate vest and rafts, (3) how to enter rafts, (4) how to lock into a hoist for helicopter pick up, and (5) the handling of safety and survival equipment. Flight departments and training centers around the world do a basic job of preparing these crew members for the extremely rare chance of a ditching, but there is an aspect of the preparation which has not been examined. Because a real time ditching training exercise is so time intensive (expensive) and not an FAA/JAR requirement very few crews have ever experienced the 45+ minute drill in the simulator. To be effective, the exercise would need actors to portray flight attendants and extra crewmembers. Also needed are actors to portray other aircraft within VHF radio range, actors for ATC and a functioning data link system if the operator uses a system. These emergency scenarios require extensive setup (envision a South Pacific crossing with multiple possible divert options). The setup time combined with required actors combined with simulator time equates to significant expenditures of training funds. See Chapter 12 for sample simulator examples.

In every industry, especially those involving machinery, two of the most important tenants of safety are PREPARATION and COMMUNICATION.

I summarize preparation for the front end crew as (a) having a working knowledge of how to handle the aircraft from power loss to water touchdown; and (b) front end crew pointing the aircraft in the right direction to either facilitate rescue, reach an area of best water conditions (beach, bay, or protected side of an island), or nearest to a surface vessel; and (c) picking the best ditching heading and (d) having basic knowledge of how to handle the last 100 feet.

Preparation for the back end crew is currently well trained. And what great training and safety attitudes they have. The 'managers in the back' can be very aggressive when time comes to put on the emergency game face. After all, they are not on the aircraft to serve drinks or food…they are there because the governing agency requires them for safety, and when an 'event' occurs they spring into action. If you have never seen a professional flight attendant directing evacuation while under stress, it is very interesting and can be very intense. Flight attendants, loadmasters, engineers, flight mechanics, and load technicians deal daily with all types of passengers and problems which is real world stress management. They are accustomed to dealing with very challenging unknowns. During a complete exercise, reinforcement of training with vest, rafts, carriers, and slides would be recommended.

How many, or perhaps a better question, have any flight attendants ever ran a ditching exercise in a 'real time' scenario where they work a full cabin to don vests, prepare rafts and secure the cabin for an offshore deep water landing? Chapter 21 gives flight training departments some ideas for improving the syllabi with a time lapsed multiple players simulator event.

Communication preparation falls into two categories: internal within the airframe, and external to the world. As important as the internal communication is for the crew and passengers, I cannot stress strongly enough the importance of external communication. You may have limited electrical power and possibility limited radios. If you are down to VHF only and the only relay aircraft within VHF radio range does not have an HF radio, or some data link capability, rescue could be delayed by hours… or days. However, if you are able to relay your location to MOM, ATC, multiple aircraft via VHF radio, and possibly even make a call direct to the correct regional rescue center (see Chapter 17), you have launched the recovery effort and greatly improved the survivability chances of all occupants.

Like buying and selling real estate, ditching is all about location, location, location! The crew is responsible to do all it can to place the aircraft as close to rescue as is possible. This is a difficult and perhaps impossible task as the crew may be so overwhelmed they may have very little input with where the ditching will occur. Should the crew be aware of their location and the best direction to head toward rescue? Absolutely. Is making that 'first turn' toward rescue the foremost thing on the crew's mind? It should be.

<u>Big Ocean Size = Time</u>

As I began research on this effort, an incredibly important fact to the googolplex power[14] began to emerge. Reality set in on an obvious fact of life. Oceans are huge (75% of the earth's surface is covered by water). And ocean crossing aircraft are airborne over them by the thousands.

---

[14] Googolplex – largest number in the world according to my kids (and Karl Sagan).

Why is this important to the googolplex power? First, the successful ditching will leave crewmembers drifting, paddling, or sailing in either the calm of beautiful seas or in the hell of rough waters…and possibly both. Second, very few aircraft plying the oceanic airways have equipment to support life more than 12 to 48 hours. Third, a search area for a ditched aircraft can easily be hundreds or thousands of square miles.

The huge expanses of the oceans equate to TIME. Even in the best scenario of continuous 406 MHz ELT hits, rescue may be days away. In the wait for maritime help, most probably a long range C-130, Nimrod or P-3 will find you to drop supplies if capable, but ships moving at a mere 20 knots will take time to reach you and pluck you from your raft or floating fuselage which has never stopped moving due to the winds and currents.

From my C-130H days I remember the longest legs being about 15 hours at 290 KTAS. So, that is maybe a range of about 4200 NM. The USCG today advertises their C-130J models have 5,500 NM range, which they use the distance of 2,000 as the radius of action with recovery at launch airport[15]. Rescue helicopters are much more limited as they boast ranges in the 420 to 660 NM range except for some that can be aerially refueled.

Here are some common routes that have significant over water stretches to illustrate the point:
Los Angeles (KLAX) to Honolulu (PHNL) – 2217 NM
New York (KLGA) to Paris (LFPB) – 3144 NM
Mexico City (MMMX) to Honolulu (PHNL) – 3293 NM
Perth (YPPH) to Chennai (VOMM) – 3391 NM
Rio de Janeiro (SBBZ) to Johannesburg (FAGC) – 3789 NM
Honolulu (PHNL) to Sydney (YSSL) – 4409 NM

---

[15] Jeff Griffin, USCG (Retired); District 13 Headquarters, interview follow up email

Melbourne (YMML) to Honolulu (PHNL) - 4789 NM
Melbourne (YMML) to Mumbai (VABB) – 5292 NM
Sydney (YSSL) to Los Angeles (KLAX) - 6509 NM

Oceans are big and search and rescue aircraft have limited range. Enough said?

Too Safe To Fail

We fly in the world of modern aircraft where we have near total faith and trust in the metal tube and sub-systems. We and our companies and insurance writers accept the low risk of ditching. And risk manager is what we all are. From a pilot's first solo to his last landing, he or she has accepted the risks of our profession. Flying aircraft across great expanses of water have been made to seem invincible. Engineering and production of today's aircraft is so effective, they seemingly cannot fail.

SIX DISASTER POSSIBILITIES

Scenario A: During a crossing the aircrew smells smoke and fumes. The immediate investigation finds the spreading white smoke and then flames from the portable 'device' such as a laptop or a video game which has been in direct sun for hours. The flames are knocked down by the halon and/or water extinguishers, but almost immediately re-generate in a much greater heat and flame producing conflagration. The heat and flames expand and the fire is out of control. Crewmembers don masks and PBEs, but the battle is lost. There is one immediate option. Ditch the airframe before it becomes a flying fireball.

Corporate airframes, freighters, and airliners all face the threat of on-board fire. Today's airliners are packed with relatively new systems including hardwired movie and entertainment systems, portable entertainment systems, hardwired Wi-Fi systems, and the newest jets have hardwired 110 volt outlets at every passenger seat. Passengers carry on entertainment systems and laptop work centers which become more advanced monthly. It is totally conceivable future technology will extend to hardwired cellular support apparatus which will bring even more wiring for antennae and power.

All of these systems contribute to what I term the 'flying electrical outlet'. On board wiring for antennae applications and distribution are low power and inherently lower risk. However, inverters, wiring, and plug-ins to supply 110 volt outlets now installed at each row of seats is an increased threat. The fire threat is reduced by the same methodology we use in airframe maintenance; re-current inspections and replacements. But, who inspects all the passenger carry-on electrical cords and devices which connect to the ship's supply and dramatically change the threat to our airframes?

Of second and major concern is the threat of battery power in all the portable music and video players and portable work centers. In normal operations the portable batteries are very low threat. But, in circumstances which are not normal (think bright sun heating lithium batteries) the batteries can become a fire threat. If you doubt this, check out the YouTube videos on lithium battery fires. The FAA has produced a battery threat video for aircrew training to show the formidable threat. It is a very serious demonstration of how the fire proliferates and can re-generate after initial extinguishment efforts.

Two very recent Boeing 747 cargo aircraft losses[16] have sent shock waves through pilots groups and the manufacturers, packers, shipper of lithium batteries. On July 27, 2011 Asiana Airline lost two pilots and the airframe in the South China Sea, and on September 3, 2010 UPS lost two pilots and the airframe in Dubai. Both crews had reported onboard fires and speculation points to lithium batteries. Regulations to change shipping requirements are being battled between pilot groups and industry as I write.

Bloomburg has published an interesting summary of the conflict between shippers and the transportation industry, "Battery-Fire Crashes Seen Every Other Year On US Flights Fought".[17]

The Bloomburg article references a September 2011 report[18] by the FAA Office of Research and Technology Development in conjunction with the United Kingdom's CAA and Transport Canada. The study focuses on potential fire threat from bulk shipment of lithium batteries and the likely number of freighter fire accidents through the year 2020. Five cargo fire incidents were identified from 1958 to 2010. The study predicts there will be 4.5 accidents due to lithium battery fires from 2011 to 2020. Read that sentence again…it is important! Shippers are challenging the report because of methodology, "un-proven fire causes", and variables used in the study.

---

[16] Wall Street Journal, July 29, 2011

[17] http:www.bloomburg.com/news2011-2012-21/battery-fire-crashes-seen-every-other-year.html

[18] http://www.fire.tc.faa.gov/pdf/11-18.pdf

To reinforce the seriousness of an un-battled fire, I reviewed the reports of Swiss Air 111[19]. On September 2, 1998 the MD-11 aircraft crashed into the bay at Blandford, Nova Scotia. The aircraft was enroute from New York JFK to Geneva, Switzerland.

The aircraft experienced a fire in the cockpit "likely started within the confines of a relatively small area above the right rear cockpit ceiling just forward of the cockpit rear wall" while cruising at Flight Level 330.

There have been many fire theories and rumors about the Swiss Air disaster and I promote none. My point of bringing up the incident is to point out how quickly a fire disaster can develop. I quote the report, "Theoretical calculations confirm that from any point along the actual flight path after the aircraft started to descend, it would not have been possible for the pilots to continue maintaining control of the aircraft for the amount of time necessary to reach the airport and complete a landing." That means the fire was growing faster than the jet could get to an airfield, and they were only 66 miles from the airport.

[19] http://www.bfu.admin.ch/common/pdf/1762_en.pdf

Scenario B: Departing Anchorage on a late night westbound flight along jet route J115, your cockpit message system comes alive with alerts of a volcanic eruption on Kiska Island. Anchorage Center is broadcasting warnings of ash growing to as high as 50,000 feet. While the cockpit crew plots coordinates and references enroute charts the windscreen lights up with a glow. Static electricity is popping along the windscreen frames. The crew begins a 180° turn to exit the ash. Engines develop heavy vibration with compressor stalls. All engines flameout. Checklists are started. Emergency descent begins as pressurization is lost. The crew struggles to communicate due to forced breathing from the oxygen system. Re-starts are having no success. The engine compressor sections are caked with the concrete-like wet ash and turbine blades are welded to the cases. The aircraft is going to ditch.

Scenario C: During a crossing you are maneuvering around thunderstorms as you relay your actions to the air traffic control. Turbulence is moderate to severe. The radar is multiple shades of red. Radio discussions on VHF radio frequency 123.45 are tense and warning. Climbing is not yet an option as the aircraft is too heavy. You maneuver to avoid cumulous cloud buildup after buildup, as hail batters the airframe. A windshield cracks. Engine vibes are off scale high. Hail intensifies. Engines flameout. Drift down begins. Re-start is attempted, but the engine damage is extreme and the engines will not re-light. The aircraft is going to ditch.

Scenario D: During a crossing, your aircraft experiences an uncontained catastrophic engine failure. Parts of the turbine section explode like shrapnel from a mortar blast and make multiple long tears on the underside of the wing and most seriously in the area of the fuel collector tank and the associated fuel pumps. Fuel is gushing overboard and the wing will be empty in minutes. You secure the engine, begin drift down, cross flow what you can, and begin computing range and making decisions on where can you go. There is not enough fuel to make an airfield. The aircraft is going to ditch.

Scenario E: Everyone on the flight line knows the mechanic as Marty. He is a quiet man of 48 years who possesses an expired passport from his 'old' country, and a shiny new US passport. He loves telling everyone about his immigration journey. He has lived in the capital city now for nine years. Marty immigrated during the days of freedom as Eastern Europe went thru the upheaval after the fall of the wall. His new start in America allowed school at a quiet aviation academy on the east coast. His entry documents were thin and unverifiable.

He worked hard at the school and fit right in with the guys and gals looking for a new start in the land of opportunity. His certificates of training as an A&P Mechanic hung on the wall inside the office of XYZ Airline. He was very proud of his 'ticket' (license) from the FAA he carried in his wallet. The ticket accredited him with power plant specialty.

This January morning was meeting the expectations of the weather forecast. Heavy overcast skies and relentless snow. Visibility on the airport ramp was reduced to 600 feet as Marty worked through the checklist for the preflight of the huge twin engine jet. Everyone on the ramp was cold and dressed from head to toe with adverse weather gear. No one paid attention to Marty, and Marty acted as if he was paying no attention to them. His tasks included checking pressures on various nitrogen bottles, oxygen bottles, and fire extinguishers. He checked oil levels for the engines, APUs and gearboxes. He stopped for a moment to help Miles the fuels handler as he worked the large hoses onto the single point refueling panel to up load some 41,000 gallons of Jet A fuel for the trip to Moscow. He said good morning to Claire the new lady driving one the four catering vans as the day's supplies of food, drinks and amenities were loaded.

But today's preflight at gate C-1 was very different. Marty is the "B" mechanic for this preflight. Aircraft crossing the oceans must be pre-flighted and inspected by two qualified mechanics. Marty worked slowly to make certain the "A" mechanic had completed his tasks and had moved on to the next jet on the schedule. Marty slipped three AA batteries into the metal box. The box, the size of a small video camera, contained a tube of sulfuric acid, potassium chlorate powder, and sugar. Chemicals that when mixed erupted into a small volcano of heat which could burn thru anything short of forged steel. Inserting the batteries started the six hour clock as the device waited to open the valves. Marty removed box #1 from his inside pocket and placed it inside the engine cowling on top of the left engine at the point where the turbine blades would spin at 15,000 revolutions per minute. He used three metal zip ties to carefully secure the device where it would stay for the next six hours.

With the heavy snow and dark skies no one could see or cared to see Marty doing his jobs. The cameras on the ramp, which would be reviewed in detail after the disaster, could not even detect his actions as he moved about the jet. As he completed his tasks on the left engine, he moved to the right engine to insert device #2. He buttoned up the engine, placed his tools in the storage locker, and worked his way upstairs into the jet way to find the aircraft forms and sign off the "B" portion of the preflight as complete. He continued his walk through the airport, with a quick stop in the men's room to remove his uniform overalls to reveal a business suit underneath. He exited the terminal, rode the escalator upstairs to re-enter security as a passenger, proceeded to gate C-12 and boarded a different international flight.

The remainder of my fictional (ready for Hollywood) story is predictable. An hour after Marty (not his real name) from his 'old' country (not his real country) completed his pre-flight, the jumbo jet pushed back from the gate with 365 passengers and 22 crew, cycled thru de-icing, and took off. Five hours later the valves in the 'devices' open, chemicals mix, and molten aluminum causes extreme vibrations in the turbine sections of the engines with subsequent catastrophic failure of both engines as the airframe passes 30° west latitude over the North Atlantic. The 520,000 pound glider has 33 minutes before it is going to land in the ocean. We have no idea of his motives…animosity for his employer; religious reasons; subterfuge from an adversarial competitor; or his grand scheme to murder someone he knew would be on the flight…but the result is the same.

Scenario F: During a polar crossing the multi-engine aircraft experiences a seemingly innocuous lightning strike while moving through scattered buildups. The lightning strike which enters at the pitot tubes on the co-pilot side of the jet below the front windows of the aircraft exits off a static wick on the elevator. The crew smells smoke which they recognize as electrical wiring. Circuit breakers begin popping on the "MAIN AC" bus. Within a minute a dozen breakers have opened. The cockpit displays flicker as power to the display units transfer from one power source to another. Tones, bells, chimes and tweets are playing a song…but no one is dancing. The electrical failure is a relatively new phenomena termed 'cascading electrical failure'. Lost are the EICAS, portions of the fault warning systems, weather radar, fuel system pumps and switching controls. And most important to the crew, lost are the fuel heater controls.

Fuel temperatures pass freezing point and approach pour point. Engine operation becomes erratic, then compressor stalls and then flameout. The aircraft begins drift down. The fuel cannot be heated quickly enough during the driftdown as the aircraft only has 32 minutes until ground contact is made. A water or ice cap landing is imminent.

Author's License

I understand that each scenario has exceptions, as some engines have shields to preclude flying turbine section parts from causing damage. Or single engine operations with one wing of fuel may have significant range to make safety, or ATC would advise a crew before they flew into volcanic ash. Or no crew would fly into a hailstorm. However, for these scenarios, there are historic examples of crews experiencing exactly what is in the scenario.

I acknowledge Scenario E is fiction. But damm scary.

I acknowledge Scenario F is partially fictional, but I use it to demonstrate the dangers of high altitude, low temperature, polar crossing flights in which fuel temperature is precariously close to freezing. It was British Airways Flight 38 (Boeing 777) on January 17, 2008 which landed short of Heathrow's runway due to ice crystals clogging the fuel-oil heat exchanger (FOHE). Boeing and Rolls Royce engineers have fixed the problem. The aircraft had been 'super cold soaked' on a 5,000 mile flight from Beijing to London.[20] Fuel temperature control demands focused attention.

I diverge from the subject of ditching for a moment to discuss cascading electrical failure to begin conversation of what can happen when software and/or hardware failures lead to reduced electrical capability. There are aviation writers who believe our industry is threatened more by the electrical complexity of modern aircraft than the threat of engine failures. The concern is driven by aircraft systems which are more and more automated to reduce 'crew workload' and manning in the cockpits. We now fly B-747s with a two man crew. We fly C-130s with two pilots and a loadmaster. The engineer career field is nearing extinction.

[20] http://www.airsafe.com/events/models/b777.htm

The technology is wonderful in day-to-day operations. However, in today's modern simulators the most common question between pilots is "why is it doing that"? This simple question is a result of the type of adopted engineering inherent in today's modern aircraft. We are faced with buttons and features in cockpits which are slaved to, or slaved from multiple other actions which can or cannot happen prior to or after another action. Cockpits of the 1960 had hundreds of switches, buttons, lights and circuit breakers. As one was turned on or off an action occurred. In our modern cockpits software determines what we see and how/why a button does what it does or won't do what we ask.

Jet jockeys of today's modern aircraft have all had moments when a message illuminates, or a chime has gone off and the pilot begins a mental search of all the sub-systems that affect that message or chime. This event can lead to maddening searches for the "why is it doing that?" I contend automated cockpits should have available to the pilots a quick reaction card detailing system to sub-system relationships. This card would be as valuable as the quick reaction checklist or whatever you call the emergency checklist.

In times of a sub-system failure or a short or fire, the automated systems can lead to cascading abnormalities which are extremely difficult to analyze. This is exactly what happened on a night sortie in December 2001 as a B1-B crashed in the Indian Ocean.[21] Aircraft control was lost at FL200 when the #1 and #2 generators fell offline followed by primary and secondary attitude instruments. The crew of four ejected the jet and lived.

---

[21] http://findarticles.com/p/articles/mi_m0UBT/is_11_17/ai_98850022/

This book is an academic drill to enhance and expand the aircrew's thinking about what happens in a ditching. And remember this guide is written for the single engine ferry pilot, corporate airframes, and large commercial passenger and freighter aircraft. Please give the scenarios due flexibility.

HISTORY OF SUCCESSFUL AIRCRAFT DITCHINGS

It is important to define the two types of ditching: inland and blue water.

Coastal, or inland ditching is defined as an attempted landing on inland waterways or along coastal areas within five miles of the shore. I use five miles for several reasons. At five miles the aircraft is visible as it is in descent and it can be reached in a relative short time from land. Fishermen, pleasure boaters, ferries, fire boats, tug boats, ski boats, jet skis, and surfers are all going to pitch in and help. There is also the possibility/capability for the crew and passengers to reach safety of the shore either by themselves or as a group and with or without flotation assistance.

Blue water ditching is defined as attempted landing more than five miles offshore and is characterized as not being seen from the land and thus rescue is not immediately launched. There is also little chance of crew or passengers immediately swimming to safety and no cavalry of boats running at full speed to rescue passengers and crew.

Below are nine examples to demonstrate an aircraft can make a successful landing on water. I include these examples to reinforce with everyone we must do some basic preparation and be ready if your luck runs out. The New York Hudson River ditching will live in our memories forever. If you are the next crew facing the oceanic landing you have to be positive! It can be done.

- On November 19, 2009 a Pel-Air medical evacuation flight (Westwind jet) enroute from Apia (in Western Samoa) to Melbourne was ditched after making several missed approaches at Norfolk Island (fuel stop) as the Westwind jet was below minimum fuel to continue flight. The flight crew of two, plus two medical crew and the passenger and spouse all evacuated the jet and were picked up by boat and brought to Norfolk. Survival rate 100%.[22]

- On January 15, 2009, US Airways Flight 1549, (an Airbus A320), ditched into the Hudson River in New York City, after reports of multiple bird strikes. All of the 155 passengers and crew aboard escaped and were rescued by passenger ferries, fire boats, police boats, and an assortment of other craft in the area. Of greatest note to most pilots was the quick and definite decision of the captain to point the airframe at the only available landing zone, the river. We all question whether we would have made the same life saving decision as quickly. Survival rate was 100%.

- On August 6, 2005, Tuninter 1153 (an ATR 72) ditched off the Sicilian coast after running out of fuel. Of 39 aboard, 20 survived with injuries including serious burns. The plane's wreck was found in three pieces. Survival rate was 59%.

- In 2002, Garuda Indonesia Flight 421 (a Boeing 737) successfully ditched into the Bengawan Solo River near Yogyakarta, Java Island after experiencing a twin engine flameout during heavy precipitation and hail. The pilots tried to restart the engines several times before making the decision to ditch the aircraft. Of the 60 occupants, one, a flight attendant, was killed. Survival rate was 98%. Photographs taken shortly after evacuation show that the plane came to rest in knee-deep water.

---

[22] www.rex.com.au

- In 1996, Ethiopian 961 (a B-767-200ER) ditched in shallow water three miles from land after being hijacked and running out of fuel. The jet impacted the water at high speed, dragging its left wingtip before tumbling and breaking into three pieces. The panicking hijackers were fighting the pilots for the control of the plane at the time of the impact, which caused the plane to roll just before hitting the water. Of 175 on board, 52 survived. Some passengers were killed on impact or trapped in the cabin when they inflated their life vests before exiting. Most of the survivors were found hanging onto a section of the fuselage that remained floating. Survival rate was 30%.

- In 1970, ALM Flight 980 (a DC-9-33CF) ditched in mile-deep water after running out of fuel during multiple attempts to land at Princess Juliana International Airport in the island of Saint Maarten in the Netherlands Antilles under low-visibility weather. Of 63 occupants, 40 survivors were recovered by U.S. military helicopters. Survival rate was 63%

- In 1963, an Aeroflot Tupolev 124 ditched into the River Neva after running out of fuel. The aircraft floated and was towed to shore by a tugboat which it had nearly hit as it came down on the water. The tug rushed to the floating aircraft and pulled it with its passengers near to the shore where the passengers disembarked onto the tug; all 52 on board escaped without injuries. Survival rate was 100%

- In 1956, Pan Am Flight 943 (a Boeing 377) ditched into the Pacific after losing two of its four engines. The aircraft was able to circle around USCGC

Pontchartrain until daybreak, when it ditched; all 31 on board survived. Survival rate was 100%

- Also in 1956, Northwest Orient Airlines Flight 2 ditched into Puget Sound after the flight engineer forgot to close the cowl gills on the Boeing Stratocruiser's engines. All aboard escaped the aircraft after a textbook landing, but four passengers and one flight attendant succumbed either to drowning or to hypothermia before being rescued. Survival rate was 87% [23]

This record is by no means all inclusive. I include these examples to offset the widespread assumption of all ditchings being fatal. Ditchings have been survivable. The survival rate is increased by the prepared crew which has had the opportunity to experience the training of the problem, and hopefully alter the disaster to a successful conclusion.

---

[23] http://www.nowpublic.com/world/airplane-water-landing-and-ditching-statistics-rates-survival

ERGO BLUE CAN SAVE YOUR LIFE AND YOUR PAX

ERGO BLUE is an application for your I-Pad or the APP is capable of being integrated into other operating systems likes Garmin, Honeywell, World Fuel, Dynon and others in the near future.

The APP is brainchild of Jim Stabile. Jim is a retired airline pilot who operates in the New York area and he began development (which has led to the creation of the Ergo Applications) back in the early 1980's as a young pilot for National Distillers Corporation in Teterboro, NJ. He is CEO of Aeronautical Data Systems. He instructed at CAE in Morristown and as of this writing he is back flying a CRJ-200 for a small airline at the ripe old age of 71. He has been working on the App for over a decade. Today, the App is perfect.

ERGO BLUE APP basics:

1. User enters coast out point (feet wet).
2. User enters coast in point (feet dry).
3. Your course is displayed on a high-quality digital world map.
4. The map displays all ships 300 miles on both sides of the route of flight. The ship locations are via multiple websites that track worldwide shipping.
5. Ships locations are updated every 15 minutes.
6. App displays offshore oil/gas platforms.

ERGO BLUE details

1. Uses GPS signal to maintain your current position.
2. Downloads internet site data to update ship location every 15 minutes.

3. Ship's information is displayed on the map and gives latitude/longitude, heading, speed, type of ship.

ERGO BLUE advanced

1. User purchases hand held maritime radio.
2. User selects maritime channel 16 (156.8) (emergency).
3. User connects radio to I-Pad.
4. User presses 'EMERGENCY' button on App and software begins transmitting aircraft position, altitude, time to touchdown, name of ship you are targeting, etc. This line-of-sight transmission hits all ships below you especially the ship you are targeting. Maritime channel 16 is constantly monitored on the bridge off all ships.

Education points for aircraft pilots:

1. Almost all boats from tugs, private yachts, cruise liners to shrimp boats to oilers to super container ships have transponders which transmit on the AIS maritime band. Very similar to what aircraft have, except maritime transponders broadcast to satellites. Satellites down link to web sites for public accessibility. Seaborne ships can broadcast this data every minute, every hour or whatever that owner wants to pay for.
2. Ships travel in straight lines whenever possible. Traffic conflicts, military restricted areas, and weather drive small, temporary diversions.
3. Only about 20% of all ocean vessels have English speakers on board.
4. If you are landing on water and you must choose between a cargo ship or a cruise ship to land alongside, well I remind you cruise ships have doctors, soft beds, good food and liquor. And low free boards which make it much easier to climb from raft to ship. Free board is particularly important when trying to retrieve people in high seas as the oscillation can be so great it could harm or kill people during the rescue.
5. If your aircraft does not have worldwide Wi-Fi to update ship locations, I refer you back to #2 above. Ergo Blue has artificial intelligence to move the ship on the map so you can find it.
6. Ergo Blue has built in hardware that if connected to a marine band handheld radio, the aircraft pilot can talk directly to the ship's pilot.

VHF aviation radios? Why do aviation radios **NOT HAVE** the capability to transmit on the VHF maritime emergency frequency (channel 16/ 156.800). It is possible! It is already being done! Coast Guard helicopters and fixed wing assets can talk with ships on the water today. We **ALL** should have that capability now! Imagine the safety enhancement of being able to talk directly to the captain on the bridge (who is now the captain who is going to rescue you and your passengers) as you are drifting down to land alongside of him or her. It takes up to 5 miles to slow/stop a ship moving at only 8-10 knots on the open water. A ship captain would have (and absolutely need) minutes to prepare for the rescue.

FORE FLIGHT – June, 25 2023 has integrated the Ergo Blue layer which is available to aircrews who want it. The Fore Flight feature is accessed by selecting the 'Send Vessels to ForeFlight box located in the upper right corner of the Ergo Blue app. This opens the ForeFlight app.

My question is who would not want it? It is a cheap insurance policy. Having ErgoBlue on the flight deck is as important as the raft in the back closet or in the overhead. I totally understand the pilot financial mind set. We spend countless hours droning along thinking about how we can save a dime. We operate with the mindset that if something is important for my job, my employer will provide it. News is, your employer is in business to save money and they… have determined the risk of you ditching is so low, you don't need Ergo Blue. But now that you know Ergo Blue exists perhaps you will change that mindset.

Sidenote: finding ships on the water during a crossing is difficult. With Ergo Blue it becomes a fun game to search and find the ships. Not to mention it lowers anxiety as the pilots know there is someone down there to help in an emergency.

HOW DO YOU LAND IN OPEN WATER?

You can do it! Movies of the last sixty years portray disabled aircraft in Category Five thunderstorms with twenty-foot swells. Why? Because drama makes movies and sells books. But it ain't like that. As you train and prepare, imagine a calm sea which you can save everyone. To go negative now defeats the entire reason for training and perpetuates the feeling of helplessness. You are not helpless!

Let's talk with the open water landing experts. Well, there aren't any. There are a few operators flying some type of float plane or amphibians. They operate around the earth as basic transport or scenic tours, but no one plans to land in open water on a regular basis. It is too dangerous for routine operations. Current operators are in protected areas for their takeoffs and landings.

I write below of a Department of Defense Operational Test & Evaluation because we spent days going out into the Atlantic. So, I can offer some guidance as to what you should expect. During these day operations, we encountered three variable conditions: calm seas, trough seas and variable sea state chop. Calm seas were fun. Trough conditions were challenging but not debilitating, rough sea state chop was horrible. The hardest task we encountered was not the landings, but the takeoffs.

CALM SEAS: In calm conditions we just landed and took off into the wind.

TROUGH SEAS: In trough conditions we always tried to land into the wind, but you cannot always find troughs aligned with current surface winds. Current surface wind is often 90°off from the direction the swells are running so you must pick which is more important. I talk more about this below in wind discussions below. Even takeoffs on swells are not terrible, but your hands and feet are doing very different pushes and pulls.

ROUGH SEA STATE CHOP: Rough Sea state chop happens when there is no overriding wind due to changing weather which results in variable and conflicting water patterns. We could land in mixed sea state but taking off was very difficult. When landing on water the aircraft is in a decreasing energy condition. It feels like the water grabs the hull or floats with heavy drag to stop it very quickly. In takeoff on water the aircraft is in an increasing energy condition. For a sea plane to takeoff the aircraft must 'get on the step' which means it accelerates to begin skimming across the water before there is enough lift from the wing to haul the aircraft into the air. In rough mixed sea state, it was very difficult to get on the step to gather enough speed to enter ground effect to lift into the air. The water was so confused and random that it was very, very rough. My last takeoff from mixed sea state was so rough that one of the flap hinges broke and I returned to Patrick AFB with a flap hanging down below the aircraft. Landing was uneventful with the good flap hinge dragging the flap along the runway. Lots of sparks, but nothing super dangerous.

THE APPROACH

As you drift down from altitude, in VMC you will have good visibility to search for that target ship you are aiming at. If IMC you are designing an instrument approach in your head so that when you pass 1,000 feet and the radar altimeter begins working you are configured for the last segment of the approach.

In the approach phase you will have unlimited distance visibility from 5,000 feet. As you pass 1,000 feet the world will seem to be closing in on you. As you pass 500 feet the world gets tighter as your peripheral vision loses references. You now can only see what is directly in front of you. When you pass 100 feet, you lose all peripheral reference and there is no more world as your vision focuses on the 'touchdown zone'.

WINDS

Winds deserve some chair flying thoughts. How are waves built? Correct - waves are constructed by the wind. Winds can be minimal, producing calm seas, to maximum producing swells as big as buildings. The number one factor to your water landing is do not hit a swell face on. It would be like landing into a brick wall. Instantaneous stop.

Disastrous. Accident investigators are taught there are two ways for an aircraft to enter water. First is slow speed ditching and second is high speed impact. They talk about high-speed impact in these terms. "Blink your eyes as fast as you can. That is about three blinks per second or one blink every one third of a second. In high-speed impact, the paint on the rudder catches up to the paint on the radome in one third of a second."

We don't want that. So, all your planning and execution on the drift down really comes down to maneuvering the aircraft to land either on top of a swell or in the trough between the swells. And to make this more complicated, swells are moving because wind is pushing them. I bring up this dynamic because in the last ten seconds prior to water touchdown, you may be doing some unorthodox maneuvers. I call the maneuver a rudder skid. You want to maintain wings level because dragging a wing would be not good. But you want to stay aligned to the swell or the trough, so you engage in a rudder dance to stay aligned. Different? Very much so. Similar to a skid, but you cannot let the wing dip.

I speak of chair flying because that is what we have. Simulators are not designed to display swells moving across open water.

MORE ON WINDS

We learn from day one of aviation training, that we land into the wind. Tailwinds are bad – increasing landing rolls, hampering controllable roll outs and increased ground speed on landing. A tailwind increases touchdown speed at a moment when we do not want to suffer impact. You want the wing to stop flying as you touch the water. It is very important to remember that as soon as the water 'grabs' the aircraft it will stop. On land we call it ground roll. That makes a water landing, the 'water run'. It will be very short and very quick. That water run doesn't care what the touchdown speed is as long as the wing has lost it's lift.

All of this is important, but if surface wind is less than ~20 knots, I don't care. Is it important, yes. But do not attempt a 180° turn to get turned into the wind. During the drift down, you set up for some sort of final. Into the wind, aligned with the swells. Alongside of a ship. That is a lot of variables in the brain. Don't let surface wind overwhelm you.

MORE FUN THAN A PILOT SHOULD HAVE

My experience was in 1991 while flying for an Air Force Operational Test and Evaluation. Two other special ops pilots and I flew two Lake Seawolf aircraft in every imaginable scenario in eastern Florida.

LA-2T (LAKE RENEGADE)

We based at Patrick AFB and our goal was to document Lake performance. Combat control members (acting as rescue swimmers) were in Zodiac boats for safety and to measure performance as we made circular takeoffs and landings, short field takeoffs and landings at various weights and conditions. We operated at night; using night vision goggles.

Pilots with sea ratings will tell you that when you are landing and the hull or floats touch the water, it is a very satisfying feeling. We were doing it in totally blacked out conditions, in fingertip formation. Imagine our euphoria!

TURN ON THE ELT!

I bring up the importance of the newer ELTs (UHF 406 MHz) to highlight ideas which you have not thought about what happens when you lean forward and flip the switch. The signal goes up to a satellite and the signal is down linked to a mission control center. The center normally deals with personal land or water-oriented locator beacons (PLBs).

For the man or woman manning a shift at the desk at the RCC who faces a beeping on the screen that is over a non-radar area, well, adrenaline may be forth coming. This is what they immediately know:

1. Your altitude. And it is slowly decreasing. A drift down rate computes to time of landing.
2. Your ground speed. Probably somewhere in the 100 to 180 knot range.
3. Your heading.
4. The serial number of the ELT.

They now become detectives or super sleuths. Match the serial number and it gives the tail number and owner. The serial number has the phone link to who registered the ELT.

They now reference anchored sea buoys. The buoys are around the world and display wind direction, wind speed, air temperature, water temperature and some give sea state. The buoys uplink to satellites and down to websites. Think about this, they now know information about your landing spot before you descend thru 10,000 feet.

Most important is actions the RCC controller can now take.

If you are going to land within range of helicopters they can launch the alert choppers. If you are not within rotary range, they can launch the fixed wing alerts (probably C-130s). Help may be on its way to you before you descend thru 5,000 feet!

There are several other actions they have. They call via SAT phone to any maritime vessel near you. Aircraft pilots may have never heard, but every ship from tugboats to shrimpers to container ships to cruise liners have transponders. These transponders broadcast directly to satellites which down link to websites The rescue control center can speak with the ship's captain to brief the emergency. Once a ship captain is directed to assist, they are obligated under maritime law to help, or they could be brought to court and face loss of license.

Or the RCC can seek assistance from any Navy ship of any country. Or (highly classified) they can talk with submarines in the area which may assist. An aircraft descending to land on the water equals ALL HANDS ON DECK!

All you did was to flip a switch. And no one has taught you this.

Until one minute ago. If you fly with another pilot, or CFI or FAA official or EASA official, please train them.

N400PW

Here is the very successful (and recent) ditching story of a Pilatus PC-12-47E being ferried from California to Australia:[24]

November 6, 2020 at approximately 1000 miles east of Hilo, Hawaii.
The aircraft seats had been removed the aircraft was fitted with aluminum tanks, pumps, valves and associated fuel lines behind the pilots.
At FL280 near the intersection ETNIC, as the pilots were changing configuration of pumps and tanks, the engine (PT6E-67XP) surged and flamed out. After several re-start attempts the crew made the ditch decision at 8,000 feet and ditched at approximately 4pm. The pilot landed in a trough between swells. The pilot reported the swells were 5 to 10 feet high and about 20 feet apart.
Crew used personal phones to take pictures (like one below).
Crew used a satellite phone to contact Oakland Center.
US Coast Guard coordinated the rescue mission. About four hours later a C-130 arrived on-scene to airdrop supplies.
An oil tanker also arrived on-scene (M/V Ariel). None of the tanker crew spoke English. The oil tanker made three passes next to the raft during the night but had no effective way of recovering the pilots. After sunrise the oil tanker departed area.
That afternoon a container ship (M/V Horizon Reliance) arrived and using rope cannons was able to on-board the pilots. They had been in raft about 22 hours.

---

24 Magazine SAFlyerFlight.com December 9, 2020

Pilatus PC-12 NGX N4000PW

BREATHABLE AIR

Assuming you do not have an APU that can provide cabin pressure, this decision must be made in minutes.

It is so important!

In your drift down situation will you 1) emergency descend to 15,000 feet so everyone can breathe or 2) will you put everyone on ship's oxygen so you can maximize drift down distance?

This requires considerable thought and should already be decided. If there is a rescue ship in sight, perhaps a quick descent it fine. However, if you need descent range to get close to an island, beach or ship, then maybe the oxygen decision is the appropriate choice.

ON THE WATER NEW THOUGHTS

In the last ten years, aircraft manufacturers (OEMs) of business jets have been installing an interesting device on the floor in front of main cabin door. These items are 'water dams'. Engineers/builders at Embraer, Cessna and others are spending dollars to install the device on light jets.

A water dam is a piece of plastic or fiberglass that is approximately 8 inches tall and approximately 24 inches wide. If the aircraft is landed on water, the dam must be raised and locked into place before the main entry door is opened. It says this in the OEM provided Aircraft Flight Manual (with no explanation).

I have been typed in both the Embraer Phenom (2017) and Cessna Latitude (2019) and both jets have water dams. In my research I discover engineers at these at the OEMs have done studies of estimated float posture. Using your knowledge of weight and balance it is easy to understand the tail-heavy float posture of jets that have rear engines, APUs in the back, hydraulic tanks and pumps, air cycle machines, and other systems in the rear of the jet. If the jet is tail heavy, perhaps the engineers are telling us the emergency window exit is the rear may not be useable. So, they have installed the water dam device to slow intrusion of water into the cabin if you must open the main door (as you throw out the raft and have passengers step onto the now open stairs).

Regarding float posture. I encourage everyone to walk about 50 feet off the wingtip of your aircraft, turn around, and ask yourself: using my knowledge of weight and balance, how would this machine sit on the water - float posture.

THE BATTLE ON THE WATER

A minute to talk about what is happening to the aircraft on the water. I break it down as a battle between the two forces: weight and buoyancy.

Weight is simply the metals, rubber, fiberglass, and other contents which are denser than water and therefore sink. Pretty straightforward.

Buoyancy is influenced by a couple of factors. Most of the buoyancy is from the air trapped in the wings. The less fuel and more air you land with, the longer the aircraft will remain on top of the water. A sealed fuselage and sealed cargo compartments will provide buoyancy but, that buoyancy will be overcome by weight as water creeps in at some point. Things influencing buoyancy are: is the outflow valve(s) closed? Are the seals of the firewall and the rear seal of the fuselage all still viable or were they damaged during the water landing? Is there a pathway for water into the fuselage via the air cycle machine and the air vents in the aircraft? And most important, are the NACA vents under the wings allowing water into the wings?

Researching ditchings over the years I find lots of photos and videos of single and light twin engine ditchings. And they all go under water the same way – the engine is pulled under first and the tail go up into the air – and the aircraft goes straight down. Weight overcame buoyancy.

In the 1940s as aircraft designers were looking for paths to get air into the aircraft for cooling of systems and humans without producing tremendous drag, the NACA vent was invented. They are often referred to as submerged vents. If you are outside of your aircraft as it is being fueled, you can smell fuel fumes. It is because fuel fumes exit from NACA vents and other safety vents below the wing. Hence the problem, once you are on the water these vents which were never designed to keep water out (they do have features to deflect/disperse rain) allow water to enter the wing and reduces buoyancy. If weight overcomes buoyancy, the aircraft sleeps with the fishes.

Below is picture/story of B-707, tail ST-APY operated by Trans Arabian Air Transport after ditching (controlled flight) into Lake Victoria Feb 3, 2000. The 1967 model 707 had 51,200 TT and was landing HTMW (Mwanza, Tanzania) at night after power outage had darkened the airport and disabled the VOR, NDB, and all lights. A portable generator re-established runway lights and crew attempted visual approach and jet landed 2 miles short. Field elevation 3,773. All five occupants lived.

Point is jet was empty (scheduled to pickup 38 tons of fish filets) and had little fuel remaining in wings. The jet had lots of excess buoyancy. It floated indefinitely until it was towed onto a sandbar. I wonder if it is still there?

THE RING OF FIRE

Ring of fire is often talked about, and I want everyone to read this story and think about what it means.

Searching an encyclopedia, one finds the ring of fire is a huge geographic area basically under the Pacific Ocean. The ring stretches from Australia to Japan up to Eastern Russia to Alaska to Western Canada to the US coast down Central America to the west coast of South America. It is made up of tectonic plates under the ocean that are 'shifting,' and it has volcanos.

January 2022

Not long ago. Repeat that: NOT LONG AGO!

Off the island of Tonga a volcano erupted under 650 feet of ocean. The eruption lasted nine minutes and fifty seconds (think really quick). The ash cloud rapidly rose to 100,000 feet. The ash cloud spread to 160 miles wide. The volcano spit out boulders which were car sized that traveled at super sonic speeds (they set off military sensors in multiple countries).

Again I emphasize: 100,000 feet, 9+50 quick, boulders and ash supersonic. Ring of fire…what if this had happened five miles off Seattle. Or LA. Or San Diego?

ADS B AFFECT ON SEARCH AND RESCUE

If you owned or flew a small aircraft in the last decade, you are familiar with the ADS timeline. Almost everyone had to purchase and get installed ADS-B OUT equipment that connected the transponder to a special designed antenna which talks to the satellites and allows TCAS equipped aircraft and ATC to "see" your aircraft with a pulse every 5-8 seconds and in some cases every second.

What we did not know at the time was how ADS would revolutionize the Search and Rescue world.

The story of ADS-B in the year 2024 is incredible. In the US, the Air Force Rescue Coordination center located at Tyndall AFB, FL is the USAF arm of SAR. They directly tie to the Civil Air Patrol's National Radar Analysis Team. What has happened in the last decade is a story of modern technology colliding with some very smart people colliding with The Company Aireon (air traffic surveillance market). Aireon is beyond amazing! Aireon's contribution in simple words is they have given Search and Rescue organizations (NRAT) a back door password protected access to search data of distress aircraft. It has already and will for the future revolutionize SAR.

AFRCC, Rescue Control Centers, and NRAT have stories that knock your socks off. In the year 2023 it required NRAT about 20 minutes to run a data request. Today it is done in four to five seconds!

I offer one hypothetical: A CFI and instrument student are working approaches to KDLS (The Dalles, Oregon). KDLS is an uncontrolled field. They are talking to Seattle Center when able, due to terrain. After three approaches Seattle does not hear from N12345 and the center controller calls the FBO to see if the aircraft has full stop landed. The FBO has not seen the aircraft in twenty minutes. Seattle makes multiple attempts to contact N12345 to no avail. Seattle center can now start procedures to engage NRAT and the aircraft location can be pinpointed in four to five seconds![25]

---

25 **https://www.aopa.org/news-and-media/allnews/2020/september/pilot/ads-b-saving-the -day**

SELF AND FORMAL TRAINING

Chair (or Hanger) Flying
Perhaps a term you have not thought about much since your early flight training days. The timeline from engine(s) failure to water contact is not the time to put a ditching plan together. Your employer or training facility probably included the very important steps of preparations for impact, cabin evacuation, water egress, and survival equipment usage. My effort here is to emphasize that during the time between the engine failures and the landing, the aircrew will be faced with dozens of difficult decisions, required actions and required communications. If you have chair flown and discussed with other crew members the questions, problems, options, ideas, duties, and fears, then you are way ahead of the problem.

I have broken this training into four phases for consideration. Each of the phases or stages should be examined and critiqued by the individual operators to determine what can be improved and how it relates to their operation and their specific aircraft.

This chapter contains dozens of questions. Two of my friends whom are international airline captains both commented to me, "don't give so many questions…give answers". Their comment caused me great anxiety. But after many reviews, I stay with questions as this guide is for all pilots flying various air frames. Everyone must ask themselves the questions and determine their own answers for their own aircraft. I hope to spark an interest in the Baron pilot going to Bermuda, the 737 crew flying Chennai to Bangkok, the C-17 from McCord AFB to McMurdo, the freighter from Cape Town to Beijing, just as much as I spark the interest in the pilots of the heaviest new metal enroute from London to Perth.

Phase One – Assessing Aircraft Capabilities

This phase is done at home or in formal training.

It involves studying details of the airframe in a light which you perhaps have not yet considered. What is no engine drift down speed at various altitudes? At glide speed, what will be the VVI? At glide speed what is the glide ratio (how many miles forward is the aircraft going to travel for each mile of descent)? Would flaps or slats enhance glide ratios, or is clean wing always the way to go? What does the glide ratio equate to in minutes? Imagine trying to explain to a back-end crewmember or a passenger the ratio is 17 to 1? All they want to know is how many minutes until the 'landing'. What are the winds doing to your glide distance?

APPROXIMATE GLIDE RATIOS[26]

Aircraft	~Ratio	~Distance Traveled With Engines Failed At 35,000 Feet[27]	~ Minutes To Landing
Space Shuttle	4.5:1	29	7
Cessna 172*	9:1	59	41
Boeing 767 (Actual From Gimli)[28]	12:1	79	34
Gulfstream IV	15:1	99	43
Boeing 747	17:1	112	48
Airbus 320	20:1	132	57
U-2	28:1	185	129
Sample Sailplane*	50:1	~331	~172

*Yes, very difficult to get either the sailplane or the single engine aircraft to FL350…but I throw them in for comparison.

The front end crew has only a few minutes to make decisions and answer the myriad of questions bombarding the cockpit from: a) radios via 121.5, 123.45, HF, ATC; b) AFIS, APIS, ADS-B in and out, CPDLC, MOM, and any other data link system the future has in store for us; c) other pilots onboard who can be summoned to assist; d) flight attendants or loadmasters in the back who are now faced with calming, training, assisting, and preparing the passengers. And quick, in your aircraft, what radios have power without engine generators?

---

26 Finding exact glide ratio numbers is not easy. One of the most difficult efforts I engaged in.

27 www.csgnetwork.com/glideratiocalc.html

28 Air Canada Flight 143, July 23, 1983, Boeing 767 landed at Gimli, Manitoba, Canada

If you have lost all engines or are crippled for whatever reason and are about to ditch, there will be all sorts of passenger problems from too many infants for the infant carriers to able bodied passengers who now have fallen apart and are no longer able and need to be re-seated. There will be heart problems, irrational problems, passengers who cannot swim, passengers worried about Fido or Fluffy in the baggage compartment, and hopefully many passengers who are helpful in calming others. This brief list is by no means all inclusive. I am sure the ocean crossing experts can send in dozens of stories which I have never even dreamed of[29]. In the mayhem, add in the excitement of pressurization loss, limited electrical buses powering only some of your radios and intercoms, and of course your emergency will occur in the hours of darkness, with heavy lightning producing CBs surface to FL 450 (we have all seen the movies).

What is the landing configuration for a ditching? Depending on your type, it may be with flaps or not. Speed brakes or not? Gear up or not? APU on or not?

If you have lost power from all engines and thus lost pressurization (assuming no APU for pressurization), will you make an emergency descent to a lower altitude with breathable air for the passengers, thus wasting valuable glide distance and preparation time, or will you put everyone on oxygen and take advantage of maximum glide range and accept the possible risk of passenger incapacitation? And if you do put everyone on oxygen, is the cabin crew prepared to use walk around bottles as they prepare the cabin for the water landing?

---

[29] Send your comments/stories to d.m.montgomery@gmail.com

If you experience high altitude loss of pressurization, and must put on a mask, you are in for a challenge. As a pilot, have you ever donned an oxygen mask and tried to talk to the other pilot or talk on the radio with forced pressure breathing in a now un-pressurized aircraft? It is not easy. The oxygen system and the mask are attempting to force oxygen into your lungs, while you are trying to communicate (talking via exhaling) with other crew or on a radio. The feeling is very distracting and diverts attention at a time when you need 100% of your attention to focus on the tasks at hand. I experienced a rapid decompression in 2004, as the glue on the main door seal failed and the door seal 'rolled outside' the jet. The wind stream pulled the entire seal from around the door, and it became a dropped object from 40,000 feet over the North Atlantic. The gap is only inches wide, but it is 18 feet long. This equals a large hole in the side of the aircraft. We began an emergency descent and donned oxygen masks. The pressure in the masks was very strong. Talking on the radio or to the other pilot was an effort to exhale against the pressure. I found that to issue guidance to the co-pilot I needed to pull the mask from my face, make a quick statement, and re-seal the mask. Obvious not desirable, but as I have said dozens of times in my career, "emergencies in the aircraft, never flow like they do in the sim."

With reduced electrical power, is your TCAS still able to display aircraft that may be below you as you start the glide (or emergency descent), and are you still being painting to other aircraft? Do you have radio capability to relay to whomever can hear your current LATITUDE/ LONGITUDE as progress continues? Is it possible to make one phone call to contact SAR immediately? (YES if your phone has power)

At what altitude can you start the APU or HMG? If the aircraft has a RAT (ram air turbine), exactly what will be powered? How long do your INS, IRS, FMS, GPS systems give accurate data after generator loss, and will that computer continue to interface with the other flight management boxes in the cockpit? Does the radar altimeter work over calm or violent water? Does the FMS/UNS/GPS give constant wind data to help you get the airframe turned into the prevailing wind? Does the on-board phone system have power without engine generators? Do you see the most pertinent question here: Do all the bells and whistles work with no electrical power from the engines?
Has your aircraft been modified with the new 406 MHz ELT? Does your ELT installation interface to the navigation systems to transmit the lat/long when activated? And what happens in the SARSAT System when a signal is received from a 406 MHz ELT? (SARSAT Systems Chapter 13).

This is a good place to discuss a needed change in pilot mentality regarding search and rescue. In the decades prior to 2005 or so, pilots believed in and relied on an electronic homing device (ELT) to activate during a crash. This device post-crash was expected to send signals to satellites, aircraft, and ground search parties who would use special receivers to locate the wreck. In the non-radar environments of over water legs, they were often little help in locating the crash if the airframe sank immediately.

But, as we forward to today, crews operating in the non-radar oceanic environment have a perfect solution to summoning help. All that is required is to flip a small ELT switch to 'ON'...which then instantly begins broadcasting the three Ws. Satellites almost immediately begin 'seeing' who, what, and where[30]. And even better, each few seconds, the 'where' is updated and SAR forces start operations with a definite search location, rather than an approximate location or even worse, no location if you have ditched and the airframe sunk.

---

[30] For 406 ELTs which have lat/long inputs from navigation systems

So, to the change in pilot mentality. In a dire situation out over the water or any non-radar airspace, do pilots have in their mind to flip the switch? Perhaps yes. But here is the worst possible historic answer. On May 31, 2009 Air France Flight 447 encountered a catastrophic situation which resulted in loss of the aircraft in the South Atlantic[31]. Scattered debris was located June 6, 2009 (6 days post loss). The wreckage (CVR and FDR and fuselage) was not discovered until May 2, 2011 (almost two years post loss). I humbly withdraw from trying to summarize the stress of the crew trying to gain control of the aircraft in their situation, but what if one of the flight deck crew had 'flipped on' the ELT? In the seconds of descent, the signal location would have hit the satellites and SAR could have been started within hours. Two years of agony for all concerned could have been greatly reduced. In my opinion, our training scenarios of non-radar operations must include 'ELT-ON' if there is any sign of a serious problem. In the case of "oops we don't need that after all", I would much rather have to write a letter of explanation the next day, than to have ditched and possibly sank before the satellites lock on to it (as was the case of AF 447[32]).

The 'what ifs' in the power loss/ditching scenario are innumerable. What if you have a massive fuel leak and one wing is full and one wing is going to be empty; is the aircraft controllable with such an imbalance? If you can dump fuel, might you dump good fuel to maintain controllability of the aircraft at touchdown?

---

[31] www.popularmechanics.com/technology/aviation/crashes/what-really-happened-aboard-air-france-447-6611877

[32] Interview Jeff Griffin, USCG (Retired) District 13 Command Center; Seattle; Mar 15, 2012

What if during the glide, you spot a surface vessel. If there is a vessel on the water, what type of 'landing pattern' are you going to fly to ensure the ship sees you and thus enhances the chance of pickup? What if it is nighttime and you want the ship to see you? This is a great chair flying exercise to think about…how would you maneuver for a downwind, base turn, and final over a ship or island?

If you are flying a cargo aircraft, can you/should you dump cargo? The list is extensive.

Phase Two - Descent and Preparation For Landing

This phase begins in self study and should be trained and reviewed in the simulators.

How will you setup the cockpit of the gliding airframe? As in who is going to fly? Does the autopilot have power and can it fly the glide and maintain drift down or best L/D airspeed in the direction you decide to go (which GREATLY reduces your workload)?

Does the FMS/UNS/GPS have direct to airport function? If it does not, do you have quick access to the four letter identifier or lat/long of Narsarsaraq, Guam, Christmas Island, Easter Island, St Johns, Lajes, etc so you can punch them in…to an FMS/UNS/GPS (if it still has power).

Did you segment your flight route on some sort of chart and mark SAR locations to make the FIRST TURN to the correct heading? This FIRST TURN is an important concept. Use the simple but effective example of being 400 miles southwest of Iceland. If you turn toward Reykjavik and start the glide, you may be able to get into the range of the helicopters (~300NM from the base[33])…versus continuing straight ahead and possibly out of the range for an earlier rescue.[34]

Without a doubt, the best decision for an appropriate first turn was made by the crew of Air Transit Flight 236 in April 2001 when they experienced total fuel exhaustion while crossing the Atlantic.[35] The reasons for running out of fuel started as a fuel line leak and were exacerbated by the crew applying the wrong procedure. But for the purposes here, it was another great example for making the correct decision when faced with the prospect of flying a glider. The crew had the great presence of mind of turning toward help versus continuing on the flight plan route. The crew dead stick landed the Airbus A-330 jet at Lajes Air Base in the Azores with 306 souls on board. Everyone lived.

---

33 NAT IGA OPS Manual - 3rd Ed V2.1.doc

34 Hypothetical example of an engine failure at FL 380, glide at 2000/FPM, glide at 200 KIAS. Remain airborne for 19 minutes while traveling 63NM. If the helicopters can reach out 300 miles, you have just made the possible life saving decision and hastened rescue.

35 http://aviation-safety.net/database/record.php?id=20010824-1

The intent with this book is to introduce advanced thinking about ditching. So, when out over the water (or any non-radar environment) and both/all engines fail or you experience a serious fire, what are the two very important things to do immediately without pause? Yes, I understand you will be running multiple checklists, but you must have these two ideas on you mind also. I have given the first step to alert SAR (ELT-ON), but there is a second very important step. This second step may or may not be on your ditching checklist.

Today most crews on an oceanic crossing are squawking 2000 in the transponder. During an emergency changing that squawk to 7700 greatly increases your chances of rapid response as most navies of the world monitor the emergency code. You never know what aircraft carrier, destroyer, cargo, fueler or other military asset is below you on the water. The code increases the number of vessels now 'looking' at you. All attention is good.

The COSPASS/SARSAT low earth orbit satellites orbit the earth every 100 minutes and by manually activating the aircraft ELT, your location is immediately known to multiple RCCs and thus the SAR process starts sooner rather than later. Every minute counts.

Building A Coast Out Briefing

All ocean crossing crews should build a coast out or feet wet briefing. There are excellent charts from the USN free websites[36] which provide invaluable information for the cockpit. The brief should include at a minimum the following:

- Flight route segmented on a chart or map to show first turn direction in case of power loss. Everyone must examine their flight planning documents as

[36] http://www.usno.navy.mil/FNMOC

first turn toward rescue may or may not be the same as a turn toward and alternate landing field. Alternates assume you will land on hard surfaces. You are now making a plan for the disaster scenario.

- Charted suggested ditching headings to cover the planned route of flight (heading bug)
- Charted pressure ridge display to cover the planned route of flight so you have an altimeter setting for the entire route. You may consider keeping (and updating every hour) this setting in the standby altimeter.
- Charted swell wave height and direction display to cover the planned route of flight
- Charted 1000 ft winds covering the planned route of flight
- Verbal discussion to reinforce with cabin crew what NOT to do with windows and doors in event of a ditching.

Here is a challenge for the flight planning dispatchers, agencies, and companies: can you provide for the ocean crossing aircrew a segmented pictorial chart with divert fields and magnetic ditching headings? All the data are available from various free web sites.

OR

Today's pilots are turning toward more usable flight information from either company provided or personally owned tablet devices. An APP needs to be developed to quickly access the Navy website to download the latest information before takeoff.
Do you have a sea state analysis?

One of the most important weather charts for the cockpit crew is the 'Magnetic Ditching Heading' for the flight route, like the one below. A quick glance at the chart gives the pilot the basic direction so he can spin the heading bug to the 'runway heading' for the ditching. Descending through night or IMC it gives you the best guess for an into the wind heading.

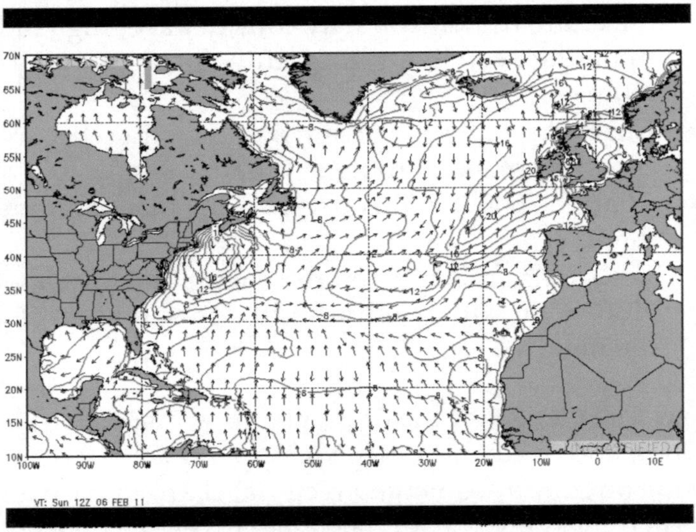

37

A second great chart is the Swell Wave Height and Direction across your flight track. Notice the correlation between swell direction and the 1000 ft winds and the ditching heading chart.

[37] http://www.usno.navy.mil/FNMOC

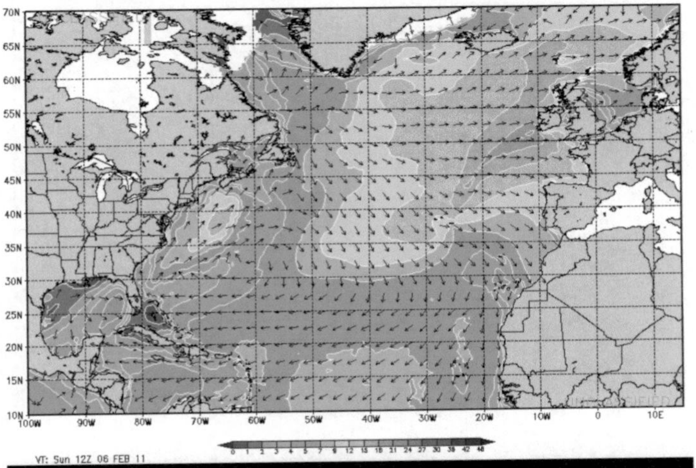

[38]

The third chart of great value to the flight crew is the Sea Level Pressure Chart like the one below. The chart gives you a good altimeter start point especially if you are descending thru IMC or nighttime.

[38] http://www.usno.navy.mil/FNMOC

[redacted]

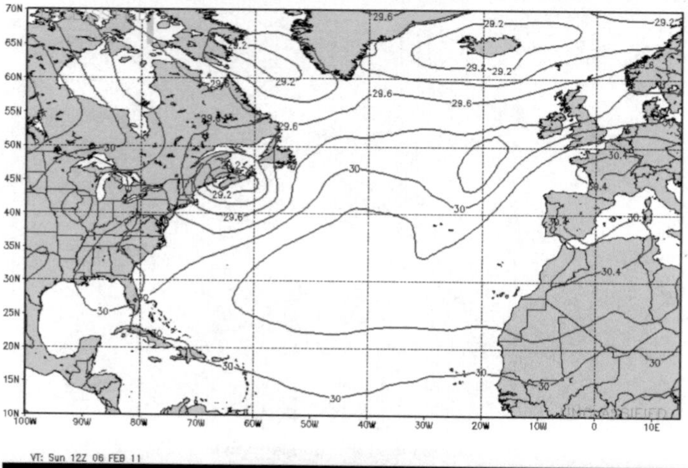

[redacted]

[39]

The predicted sea state conditions may not be exact, but every piece of information is gold. Surface wind direction and speeds aid in the setup for lowest possible groundspeed at touchdown. Altimeter settings translate into altitude awareness as you descend thru the night or IMC conditions.

I want to reiterate these charts are free from the USN website and they cover all the earth. And they are available as future prognosis so if you are 'overwater' tomorrow, you can get a printout at home the night prior.

<u>Phase Three - The Last Thousand Feet</u>

---

[39] http://www.usno.navy.mil/FNMOC

From the minute when your cozy cocoon turned into a heavier than air glider, the dozens of decisions have now funneled down to only a few more. We have all seen video of a large jet touch down on calm water and decelerate to a stop without breaking up. Water landings can be made successfully if the conditions are tolerable, pilot technique is good, and the basic rules of flight are adhered to. Hopefully in the descent you have broken out of IMC and can begin to make analysis of what the water and wind are doing. This will be the minute or two for you to get the airframe aligned into the wind, set up for touchdown in a trough, or on a swell, or whatever you pick.

My Navy buddies all have great doubts about the success of blue water landings. Their fears and doubts stem from knowledge gathered in years of sea duty watching swell patterns and sea chop which can be deceivingly mixed up. Swells were started by the wind hundreds of miles from where you are now, where as white caps are a better indicator of the current wind. And this is a landing you don't get to practice for. One shot is hopefully all you get in your career. If you own or have access to published data from various airframe manufacturers you can gather information for your plan. Of course, operators should fly their aircraft in accordance with their Flight Operations Manual, the Aircraft Operations Manual, the DASH-1, the NATOPS, or whatever they use as direction and instruction for flying the aircraft. Knowledge is power; read all you can. Professional pilots rely on memories they have built on years of experience. It is what gives them the skill to land on center line, on speed, in a 25 knot crosswind with RVR 2400. Reviewing various aircraft manufacturer data on ditching helps each pilot make their own plan.

Here is a challenge to the 'training industry' of the aviation community. Simulators should provide water landing training. To be realistic, we need a visual system to reproduce (a) glassy water, (b) symmetrical swell patterns, and (c) mixed chop and swells. And the software is needed to simulate how the aircraft reacts to each type of sea state under day/night low visibility conditions. Perhaps much of the sea state software is already written for the training of a large ship's crews in the maritime simulators. Is this complex and expensive? Absolutely. Does the industry need it? Absolutely. Will the first training center to perfect it take a huge advertising lead? Absolutely. See Chapter 21 for a generic simulator example.

Phase Four - The Last 100 Feet

Make or break? Skill or luck? Success or failure? The answers will greatly favor success by the pilots who have studied and mentally prepared for this last 100 feet. The touchdown will be factored by wind analysis, proper airframe configuration, and last second decisions. Into the wind is obvious but may not be possible due to swell alignment. Lowest possible ground speed equates to less energy which must be dissipated in the contact with the water.

If I can summarize the priorities of a water landing:

- Do not destroy the airframe by landing into the face of a large swell.
- Do not attempt to land too fast or too slow.
- Maneuver the airframe to the top or the back of the swell or to the trough.

This is a landing totally different from the flare and touchdown on the 7000 feet strip of concrete. This landing is all about placing the airframe in a touchdown attitude to take advantage of minimal energy. This minimal energy equates to the lessening of the brute force of impact. And rest assured, the touchdown on a sea of gently rolling swells, or massive mixed chop has the potential to be very brutal.

In reviewing manufacturer's data from several aircraft manufacturers, the recurrent theme is to land parallel to the waves and swells. The data also talks about landing on the windward side of those swells. To me the words are confusing. In the heat and pressure of a ditching, I do not think I could define windward or leeward. But, as you keep in mind the general surface wind direction, and point basically in that direction, you will have a minute to look at those swells and decide to either land on the right side or the left side. That is about as simple as I can make it. New Chapter 4 gives more techniques.

If approach is too slow, and the airframe is stalled and pancaked in, results will not be good. Water can be as hard as concrete…you have to trust me on this one. Also if the approach is too slow and rudder or elevator effectiveness is lost, you risk roll and wing tip impact. Another bad outcome. Enough said about too slow. Too slow is bad.

Too fast is equally deadly. A too fast approach and attempted touchdown may result in a skip or bounce leaving the aircraft in the situation of being airborne again below minimum controllable speed which decreases the advantage of you picking the landing spot versus the aircraft running out of flying speed and picking it's own spot. See too slow words above.

Too fast also means subjecting the airframe to unneeded and potentially catastrophic stresses. Fuselage and wing attach bolts and systems are obviously very strong. Strong enough to withstand years of turbulence and landing stresses. But water contact stress is immense, and the pilot flying must strive to allow the airframe to 'settle' into the water at the ideal minimum speed.

In offshore landings, one of the hardest tasks is to pick the touchdown spot. At 120 KIAS you are covering two miles per minute, or ~2500 feet every 15 seconds. From 1000 feet above the water, you can see a fair distance, but as descent continues the field of vision narrows to a few thousands of feet. And narrowing is exactly what I mean. In the descent you have forward and peripheral vision. Each 100 feet lower the peripheral gets smaller, smaller and smaller to the point where all you can see is the ocean directly in front of you. In the offshore environment, as the aircraft nears the water below 100 feet, I often had the very distinct feeling of settling into a hole, which is caused by the combination of loss of forward vision, and loss of peripheral vision, and it is even more exaggerated if there is any swell action around the aircraft that obscures your view of the horizon.

Unless the seas are glassy or the swells are wide, symmetrical, and long, the landing spot is elusive. As I made multiple offshore landings in a mixed chop sea state, my brain was constantly saying to me, "that looks good… no that looks better… no, over there looks better, wait the best is over there". A pitching sea is the total and complete ultimate state of confusion. So, the pilot at the controls has about fifteen seconds as the aircraft enters ground effect in the touchdown speed range, to make the decision of where to put the aircraft.

I cannot over emphasize the concept of speed and the dissipation of energy. Think of it like this. If reference speed (approach speed) is 1.3 times the stall speed (realizing different airframes use different definitions and/or factors), then a 150 KIAS ref speed equates to a 115 KIAS stall speed. A 35 KIAS difference. The difference of touching down at 150 as opposed to stall speed + 5 at 120 KIAS (or even stall speed -5 knots) is huge. Every knot of energy (I know we don't measure energy in KIAS, but you follow what I mean) equates to violence as the total energy at touchdown is going to very rapidly reduce to zero energy as the airframe stops. The airframe will decelerate in seconds. The engineers out there can look at the video of the landing in the Hudson River and evaluate the weight of the jet with touchdown speed and influence of the wind and compute energy loss (KIAS) per second which will give us 'ground roll', or water roll if you will. There is a YouTube video[40] of a WWII B-29 performing a ditching in the Pacific Ocean alongside the sea plane tender the USS Bering Strait. The bomber holds what appears to be a perfect landing attitude. Upon touchdown the bomber's water run is one aircraft length! The pilot, Captain Barney McCaskill, broke his back during the landing. That is deceleration! During water landings, the pilots of amphibians and float planes have the sensation of the water 'grabbing' the airframe. The feeling is due to the much greater rate of dissipation of energy versus a wheels landing on pavement. A similar example of this sensation is landing with zero headwind versus a landing with a 50 knot headwind, but it is much more exaggerated with the high drag of the water contact.

---

[40] http://www.youtube.com/watch?v=Cme9JcdSepA&feature=related

The ditching was March 9, 1945 as the United States launched 300 bombing aircraft to strike Tokyo. The mission was 3000 miles round trip and fuel was cut to bare minimum to increase bomb capacity. Many aircraft could not make it back to bases because of wind, etc.

More thoughts on the landing:

- Wind screens may burst. Consider donning goggles and oxygen mask and jackets.
- If yoke is mechanically attached to flight controls, it may whip forward or backward.
- G forces from deceleration and/or wave impact will be high. Lock seat belts and possibly use pillows or cushions to protect the head, legs and torso.
- Aircraft with under wing engines have a special challenge. In a ditching, the engines are now speed brakes, or better defined as water brakes. The engines must be put into the water at the same time to avoid extreme yaw and possible cartwheeling.
- APU/ RAT on or off?
- You should verbally reinforce with the cabin crew (and possibly passengers via a PA) to NOT open any hatches or doors until they are sure the exit is above the water line. Only after the airframe stops forward movement and the center of gravity establishes the float posture, should the determination be made to open any exit. Extreme caution must be used to not make a very bad situation much worse. This concept goes against old school training directives to open all doors and hatches before impact so you are assured, they will not be twisted or jammed from the crash. I propose that an aircraft ditching in blue water in the wide-open ocean with the potential to be on the water for an extended time should NOT open hatches or doors prior to landing. The threat of water invasion is much greater than the threat of one or more jammed windows or doors. In today's modern aircraft, the risk of a jammed window or door, is minimalized by the multiple other exits to utilize.
- Should you manually close the outflow and/or safety valves to slow water flow into the airframe?

- Should the Captain have the First Officer or Co-Pilot and extra pilots go sit in the back assuming cockpit survival has a decreased chance of survival? How valuable is a second pilot on the flight deck versus having another highly trained person in the raft who knows the raft equipment and can enhance survival? A very tough decision and order to give.
- Water landings have a great potential for extreme violence. I once broke a flap hinge on landing in rough chop. Anything and everything which is not tied down, should be stowed. This includes cockpit and cabin.
- Suppose you are ditching an airframe which is on fire or almost out of gas. Do you land with an engine(s) running? Or should you shut it/them down just prior to landing? Remember that scene from the movie[41]? Obviously, an engine will not run very long after submersion in water. But what you should think about is if you land on/in the water with engine(s) running and the compressor and turbine sections (or propellers) are instantly (within seconds) stopped, the chance of an uncontained explosion will increase. This adds massive confusion to crew and passengers and increases risk to the integrity of the hull. You must consider configuring the jet and shutting down any running engine(s) prior to water contact.

I would be remiss if I did not mention glassy water situations. I recently made a South Pacific crossing and for three hours the winds at all altitudes were zero to five knots. The surface winds were calm. The surface of the water was totally reflective in all directions, so oceanic glassy water does happen.

---

[41] Castaway; December 2000. 20th Century Fox

During the training and standards ride for a sea plane rating one event the examinee must demonstrate is a glassy water approach and landing. The simple reason is: THEY ARE DANGEROUS. The general approach for glassy water is to configure the aircraft, set up the proper (minimal) descent rate, set minimal power, and just hold that picture. The danger is glassy water is reflective. Reflective means you cannot judge height and thus…well you get the picture. If you are gliding an airframe and the water is reflective, you are going to have to carefully monitor the VVI as you maneuver to reach desired landing speed. You are going to have to use all skills to attain touch down speed in the same ten seconds that you hold 100 to 200 VVI. A functioning radar altimeter that works over water is a huge advantage. Odds are in your career you won't ever be making an engine out glider approach to blue water. And the odds are tremendously higher the water will not be glassy, but just in case it is, you are forewarned. File this in the neat to know file.

ETOPS

Some words and definitions about ETOPS (Extended Range Twin Engine Operations Performance Standards). I throw this basic introduction in just for the knowledge and training value, building more on your doctorate. ETOPS has little to do with SAR, unless the odds catch up with you. If you are a commercial operator with years of experience, this stuff is old hat.

If you are new to this genre, you may wonder how government regulators around the world have come to agree and regulate the operation of multi-engine aircraft over the seas. ETOPS programs are the answer. Without an ETOPS rating, an aircraft with only two engines must be able to get to an airport where it can safely land within XX minutes if an engine fails in-flight. ETOPS extends this "rule time" to 90 minutes or more, up to a maximum of 370 minutes (2024 - certified aircraft and crew).

Obtaining an ETOPS rating requires certification of the reliability of an airframe/engine combination as well as certification of the flight and maintenance departments. Suitable divert fields (and their weather) also play a major role in determining what routes and airframes attain ETOPS ratings. Usually, extra equipment is required as well, such as additional backup systems for electrical power. ETOPS does not require over-water equipment (e.g., life rafts) or additional fuel tanks, though these are usually required for the typical missions of ETOPS-rated aircraft.[42]

[42] http://gc.kls2.com/faq.html#$etops

So, in simple layman terms ETOPS is a risk mitigation tool. Assuredly it is a very complicated and expensive tool. It requires the crew to have extra training and the machine to have enough redundancy to greatly increase the chance the aircraft will make it safely to land if an engine fails while over water or over the poles. The range has gradually increased over time as engine and airframe reliability continuously improve. As airframes go thru certification, they demonstrate engine out capability during proving flights. Technical data is recorded for measuring and publication. Statistics such as in-flight engine shutdowns per 100,000 hours are very significant in the certification process. Today the FAA says turbine engines fail at a rate 1 every 375,000 hours while piston engines fail at the rate of 1 every 3,200.

While working on this guide, the FAA is constantly reviewing changes to the rules. The operators on polar routes have requested and seem to be close to receiving authorization to operate 6+ hours (nicknamed the 370 rule) from suitable divert fields. Some aircraft/ engine combinations are posting incredible numbers

Acronyms can sometimes be very serious, or comically twisted:
ETOPS can also mean
Engines Turn Or People Swim.

Before I end this chapter, I must put in an advertisement for the sea plane rating. It is one of the greatest experiences of your aviation education. It does not equate to being in the delivery room as your child is born, but each time you hear the sssssshhhhhh as the hull or floats find the water it will bring a smile to your face. You can wear shorts and tennis shoes and make touch and goes on some of the most beautiful lakes and rivers and bays in the country. It is one of the best training events I have ever undergone and a great way to expand your Doctorate Degree in Aviation. After the training you will never cross water again without looking down and analyzing what is happening on the surface.

Below is the official FAA approach to ditching derived from the AERONAUTICAL INFORMATION MANUAL[43]

Section 3. Distress and Urgency Procedures

6−3−1. Distress and Urgency Communications

a. A pilot who encounters a distress or urgency condition can obtain assistance simply by contacting the air traffic facility or other agency in whose area of responsibility the aircraft is operating, stating the nature of the difficulty, pilot's intentions and assistance desired. Distress and urgency communications procedures are prescribed by the International Civil Aviation Organization (ICAO), however, and have decided advantages over the informal procedure described above.

b. Distress and urgency communications procedures discussed in the following paragraphs relate to the use of air ground voice communications.

c. The initial communication, and if considered necessary, any subsequent transmissions by an aircraft in distress should begin with the signal MAYDAY, preferably repeated three times. The signal PAN−PAN should be used in the same manner for an urgency condition.

[43] Department of Transportation, Federal Aviation Administration, Aeronautical Information Manual, Change 1, August 26, 2010

d. Distress communications have absolute priority over all other communications, and the word MAYDAY commands radio silence on the frequency in use. Urgency communications have priority over all other communications except distress, and the word PAN–PAN warns other stations not to interfere with urgency transmissions.

e. Normally, the station addressed will be the air traffic facility or other agency providing air traffic services, on the frequency in use at the time. If the pilot is not communicating and receiving services, the station to be called will normally be the air traffic facility or other agency in whose area of responsibility the aircraft is operating, on the appropriate assigned frequency. If the station addressed does not respond, or if time or the situation dictates, the distress or urgency message may be broadcast, or a collect call may be used, addressing "Any Station (Tower) (Radio) (Radar)."

f. The station addressed should immediately acknowledge a distress or urgency message, provide assistance, coordinate and direct the activities of assisting facilities, and alert the appropriate search and rescue coordinator if warranted. Responsibility will be transferred to another station only if better handling will result.

g. All other stations, aircraft and ground, will continue to listen until it is evident that assistance is being provided. If any station becomes aware that the station being called either has not received a distress or urgency message, or cannot communicate with the aircraft in difficulty, it will attempt to contact the aircraft and provide assistance.

h. Although the frequency in use or other frequencies assigned by ATC are preferable, the following emergency frequencies can be used for distress or urgency communications, if necessary or desirable:

1. 121.5 MHz and 243.0 MHz. Both have a range generally limited to line of sight. 121.5 MHz is guarded by direction finding stations and some military and civil aircraft. 243.0 MHz is guarded by military aircraft. Both 121.5 MHz and 243.0 MHz are guarded by military towers, most civil towers, FSSs, and radar facilities. Normally ARTCC emergency frequency capability does not extend to radar coverage limits. If an ARTCC does not respond when called on 121.5 MHz or 243.0 MHz, call the nearest tower or FSS.

2. HF radio frequency 2182 kHz. The range is generally less than 300 miles for the average aircraft installation. It can be used to request assistance from stations in the maritime service. 2182 kHz is guarded by major radio stations serving Coast Guard Rescue Coordination Centers, and Coast Guard units along the sea coasts of the U.S. and shores of the Great Lakes. The call "Coast Guard" will alert all Coast Guard Radio Stations within range. 2182 kHz is also guarded by most commercial coast stations and some ships and boats.

6–3–2. Obtaining Emergency Assistance

a. A pilot in any distress or urgency condition should immediately take the following action, not necessarily in the order listed, to obtain assistance:

1. Climb, if possible, for improved communications, and better radar and direction finding detection. However, it must be understood that unauthorized climb or descent under IFR conditions within controlled airspace is prohibited, except as permitted by 14 CFR Section 91.3(b).

2. If equipped with a radar beacon transponder (civil) or IFF/SIF (military):
(a) Continue squawking assigned Mode A/3 discrete code/VFR code and Mode C altitude encoding when in radio contact with an air traffic facility or other agency providing air traffic services, unless instructed to do otherwise.
(b) If unable to immediately establish communications with an air traffic facility/agency, squawk Mode A/3, Code 7700/Emergency and Mode C.

3. Transmit a distress or urgency message consisting of as many as necessary of the following elements, preferably in the order listed:

(a) If distress, MAYDAY, MAYDAY, MAYDAY; if urgency, PAN–PAN, PAN–PAN, PAN–PAN.
(b) Name of station addressed.
(c) Aircraft identification and type.
(d) Nature of distress or urgency.
(e) Weather.
(f) Pilots intentions and request.
(g) Present position, and heading; or if lost, last known position, time, and heading since that position.
(h) Altitude or flight level.
(i) Fuel remaining in minutes.
(j) Number of people on board.
(k) Any other useful information.

b. After establishing radio contact, comply with advice and instructions received. Cooperate. Do not hesitate to ask questions or clarify instructions when you do not understand or if you cannot comply with clearance. Assist the ground station to control communications on the frequency in use. Silence interfering radio stations. Do not change frequency or change to another ground station unless absolutely necessary. If you do, advise the ground station of the new frequency and station name prior to the change, transmitting in the blind if necessary. If two-way communications cannot be established on the new frequency, return immediately to the frequency or station where two-way communications last existed.
c. When in a distress condition with bailout, crash landing or ditching imminent, take the following additional actions to assist search and rescue units:

1. Time and circumstances permitting, transmit as many as necessary of the message elements in subparagraph a3 above, and any of the following that you think might be helpful:
(a) ELT status.
(b) Visible landmarks.
(c) Aircraft color.
(d) Number of persons on board.
(e) Emergency equipment on board.

2. Actuate your ELT if the installation permits.

3. For bailout, and for crash landing or ditching if risk of fire is not a consideration, set your radio for continuous transmission.

4. If it becomes necessary to ditch, make every effort to ditch near a surface vessel. If time permits, an FAA facility should be able to get the position of the nearest commercial or Coast Guard vessel from a Coast Guard Rescue Coordination Center.

5. After a crash landing, unless you have good reason to believe that you will not be located by search aircraft or ground teams, it is best to remain with your aircraft and prepare means for signaling search aircraft.

6−3−3. Ditching Procedures

See the FAA Airman's Information Manual for diagrams on ditching.

a. A successful aircraft ditching is dependent on three primary factors. In order of importance they are:
1. Sea conditions and wind.
2. Type of aircraft.
3. Skill and technique of pilot.

b. Common oceanographic terminology.
1. Sea. The condition of the surface that is the result of both waves and swells.
2. Wave (or Chop). The condition of the surface caused by the local winds.
3. Swell. The condition of the surface which has been caused by a distance disturbance.
4. Swell Face. The side of the swell toward the observer. The backside is the side away from the observer. These definitions apply regardless of the direction of swell movement.
5. Primary Swell. The swell system having the greatest height from trough to crest.

6. Secondary Swells. Those swell systems of less height than the primary swell.
7. Fetch. The distance the waves have been driven by a wind blowing in a constant direction, without obstruction.
8. Swell Period. The time interval between the passage of two successive crests at the same spot in the water, measured in seconds.
9. Swell Velocity. The speed and direction of the swell with relation to a fixed reference point, measured in knots. There is little movement of water in the horizontal direction. Swells move primarily in a vertical motion, similar to the motion observed when shaking out a carpet.
10. Swell Direction. The direction from which a swell is moving. This direction is not necessarily the result of the wind present at the scene. The swell may be moving into or across the local wind. Swells, once set in motion, tend to maintain their original direction for as long as they continue in deep water, regardless of changes in wind direction.
11. Swell Height. The height between crest and trough, measured in feet. The vast majority of ocean swells are lower than 12 to 15 feet, and swells over 25 feet are not common at any spot on the oceans. Successive swells may differ considerably in height.

c. In order to select a good heading when ditching an aircraft, a basic evaluation of the sea is required. Selection of a good ditching heading may well minimize damage and could save your life. It can be extremely dangerous to land into the wind without regard to sea conditions; the swell system, or systems, must be taken into consideration. Remember one axiom– AVOID THE FACE OF A SWELL.

1. In ditching parallel to the swell, it makes little difference whether touchdown is on the top of the crest or in the trough. It is preferable, however, to land on the top or back side of the swell, if possible. After determining which heading (and its reciprocal) will
parallel the swell, select the heading with the most into the wind component.

2. If only one swell system exists, the problem is relatively simple – even with a high, fast system. Unfortunately, most cases involve two or more swell systems running in different directions. With more than one system present, the sea presents a confused appearance. One of the most difficult situations occurs when two swell systems are at right angles. For example, if one system is eight feet high, and the other three feet, plan to land parallel to the primary system, and on the down swell of the secondary system. If both systems are of equal height, a compromise may be advisable – select an intermediate heading at 45 degrees down swell to both systems. When landing down a secondary swell, attempt to touch down on the back side, not on the face of the swell.

3. If the swell system is formidable, it is considered advisable, in landplanes, to accept more crosswind in order to avoid landing directly into the swell.

4. The secondary swell system is often from the same direction as the wind. Here, the landing may be made parallel to the primary system, with the wind and secondary system at an angle. There is a choice to two directions paralleling the primary system. One direction is downwind and down the secondary swell, and the other is into the wind and into the secondary swell, the choice will depend on the velocity of the wind versus the velocity and height of the secondary swell.

d. The simplest method of estimating the wind direction and velocity is to examine the wind streaks on the water. These appear as long streaks up and down wind. Some persons may have difficulty determining wind direction after seeing the streaks on the water. Whitecaps fall forward with the wind but are overrun by the waves thus producing the illusion that the foam is sliding backward. Knowing this, and by observing the direction of the streaks, the wind direction is easily determined. Wind velocity can be estimated by noting the appearance of the whitecaps, foam and wind streaks.

1. The behavior of the aircraft on making contact with the water will vary within wide limits according to the state of the sea. If landed parallel to a single swell system, the behavior of the aircraft may approximate that to be expected on a smooth sea. If landed into a heavy swell or into a confused sea, the deceleration forces may be extremely great – resulting in breaking up of the aircraft. Within certain limits, the pilot is able to minimize these forces by proper sea evaluation and selection of ditching heading.

2. When on final approach the pilot should look ahead and observe the surface of the sea. There may be shadows and whitecaps – signs of large seas. Shadows and whitecaps close together indicate short and rough seas. Touchdown in these areas is to be avoided. Select, and touchdown in any area (only about 500 feet is needed), where the shadows and whitecaps are not so numerous.

3. Touchdown should be at the lowest speed and rate of descent which permit safe handling and optimum nose up attitude on impact. Once first impact has been made, there is often little the pilot can do to control a landplane.

e. Once pre-ditching preparations are completed, the pilot should turn to the ditching heading and commence let-down. The aircraft should be flown low over the water, and slowed down until ten knots or so above stall. At this point, additional power should be used to overcome the increased drag caused by the nose up attitude. When a smooth stretch of water appears ahead, cut power, and touchdown at the best recommended speed as fully stalled as possible. By cutting power when approaching a relatively smooth area, the pilot will prevent overshooting and will touchdown with less chance of planing off into a second uncontrolled landing. Most experienced seaplane pilots prefer to make contact with the water in a semi-stalled attitude, cutting power as the tail makes contact. This technique eliminates the chance of misjudging altitude with a resultant heavy drop in a fully stalled condition. Care must be taken not to drop the aircraft from too high altitude or to balloon due to excessive speed. The altitude above water depends on the aircraft. Over glassy smooth water, or at night without sufficient light, it is very easy, for even the most experienced pilots to misjudge altitude by 50 feet or more. Under such conditions, carry enough power to maintain nine to twelve degrees nose up attitude, and 10 to 20 percent over stalling speed until contact is made with the water. The proper use of power on the approach is of great importance. If power is available on one side only, a little power should be used to flatten the approach; however, the engine should not be used to such an extent that the aircraft cannot be turned against the good engines right down to the stall with a margin of rudder movement available. When near the stall, sudden application of excessive unbalanced power may result in loss of directional control. If power is available on one side only, a slightly higher than normal glide approach speed should be used. This will insure good control and some margin of speed after leveling off without excessive use of power. The use of power in ditching is so important that when it is certain that the coast cannot be reached, the pilot should, if possible, ditch before fuel is exhausted. The use of power in a night or instrument ditching is far more essential than under daylight contact conditions.

1. If no power is available, a greater than normal approach speed should be used down to the flare-out. This speed margin will allow the glide to be broken early and more gradually, thereby giving the pilot time and distance to feel for the surface – decreasing the possibility of stalling high or flying into the water. When landing parallel to a swell system, little difference is noted between landing on top of a crest or in the trough. If the wings of aircraft are trimmed to the surface of the sea rather than the horizon, there is little need to worry about a wing hitting a swell crest. The actual slope of a swell is very gradual. If forced to land into a swell, touchdown should be made just after passage of the crest. If contact is made on the face of the swell, the aircraft may be swamped or thrown violently into the air, dropping heavily into the next swell. If control surfaces remain intact, the pilot should attempt to maintain the proper nose above the horizon attitude <u>by rapid and positive use of the controls.</u>

f. After Touchdown. In most cases drift, caused by crosswind can be ignored; the forces acting on the aircraft after touchdown are of such magnitude that drift will be only a secondary consideration. If the aircraft is under good control, the "crab" may be kicked out with rudder just prior to touchdown. This is more important with high wing aircraft, for they are laterally unstable on the water in a crosswind and may roll to the side in ditching.

SARSAT SYSTEMS AND RESCUE ASSETS

Search and rescue in recent times was focused on the emergency frequencies 121.5 and 243.0 (UHF/military) which were activated by G forces during a crash. The frequencies were monitored by multiple satellites orbiting the globe and in turn by ground based mission control centers. During the orbits around the globe, the orbiting satellites would mark the 'hits' of the 121.5 and 243.0 emergency locator transmitters. After several passes, the mission control centers could triangulate the information and compute an area of interest which search forces could be launched to begin investigation. In the case of maritime distress, the Coast Guards would be alerted.

For inland searches in the United States (other countries have similar services) the Civil Air Patrol would be notified of the ELT. Each of the states manage and operate their own CAP Wing, and in various cities there are CAP Squadrons or Flights. Squadrons have equipment ranging from ground search trucks to aircraft equipped with radios which could electronically help in the search of the transmitting ELT.

Problem was, the electronic help in searching for the ELTs was not an exact science. Truth is, it was very difficult at least. During a crash there are multiple problems influencing the old ELT transmitters. Some would be demolished during the crash. Some would not activate. Some would be 'shielded' by debris from the crash and emit their signal in a direction which could confuse the search equipment. Sometimes ELT signals would bounce off the walls of surrounding terrain and confuse the search equipment. It was a great beginning, but technology has vastly changed and improved.

Even as the search system had problems and deficiencies, the hundreds of engineers and control center employees, and the thousands of CAP volunteers, Coast Guards, and other organizations around the world deserve huge credit as their efforts saved thousands of lives. Each geographic area operates multiple training exercises each year and the paid employees and volunteers give thousands of hours of their time to improve their skills. The rescue statistics since 1982 are very significant. Worldwide, 30,800 people have been saved. 6,600 souls were in the United States. In 2024 in the US, the Civil Air Patrol is credited with 60 saves while flying 101,000 flight hours in their 540 aircraft.

The worldwide search and rescue system changed on February 1, 2009 as the satellites and rescue control centers stopped processing radio signals from the 121.5 frequency. Control centers today have switched to monitoring the 406 MHz ELTs only. This move will allow great reductions in wasted dollars on false hits, while providing much more rapid response to accurately located distressed aircraft, ships, and hikers.

The beacons operating on 406 MHz digitally encode information such as the user registration, home address, beacon type, country of origin, number of the maritime vessel, aircraft tail number and serial number and most important, the exact location if the beacon incorporates GPS data. There are more than 990,000 406 MHz beacons operating today and the International Beacon Registration Database has registered more than 10,500 beacons from 80 countries.

How the system functions today

When a life-threatening event happens and the 406 MHz transmitters on aircraft, ships, or carried by personnel engaged in fishing, mountaineering, back country hiking, or other similar activity is activated. The signal is received by one or more of the satellites and re-transmitted to the 58 un-staffed ground stations called Local User Terminals (LUT) located in 45 countries around the world. The alert signal is then transmitted to a Mission Control Center in the country that operates the LUT. After the signal is validated, the information is transferred to the Rescue Control Center (RCC). In the US, RCCs are operated by the Air Force Rescue Coordination Center at Tyndall AFB, Florida. Other countries are briefly discussed below. The Coast Guard coordinates and conducts maritime SAR missions from one of the 16 Command Districts located in the Conus US, Puerto Rico, Guam, and Alaska. The overall manager of the US portion of the COSPAS-SARSAT system is the NOAA SARSAT office in Suitland, Maryland where the US Mission Control Center is also located.

[44]The system uses two different types of satellites: polar-orbiting satellites in low-earth orbit (LEO of which there are ~58) and satellites in geosynchronous orbit (GEO of which there are ~19). Russia and the United States provide the LEO satellite platforms. Canada, France, Russia, and the United States contribute components. The Russian NADEZHDA navigation satellites carry the COSPAS repeater packages, and NOAA weather satellites carry SARSAT packages. The NOAA LEO satellites orbit the Earth every 100 minutes. COSPAS satellites complete an orbit every 105 minutes.

The four GEO satellites continually view large areas of the Earth and can provide immediate alerting and identification of 406 MHz beacons. Even though GEO satellites cannot determine a beacon's exact location using Doppler processing, the near instantaneous alerting, user ID, and detective work by the RCC often yield the location of the distress call. Based on this information alone, search planning can begin. A SARSAT or COSPAS LEO satellite will over fly the beacon shortly and calculate a Doppler-determined exact location.

The COSPAS-SARSAT LEO system uses two modes of operation. In the repeater mode, the Search and Rescue Repeater, or SARR, immediately retransmits received beacon signals to any LUT in the satellite's footprint. This mode is possible when the spacecraft is visible to both the beacon and the ground station simultaneously, an area approximately 2,500 miles (4,000 km) in diameter. In the Store and Forward Mode, the on-board processor, or SARP, receives and records search and rescue beacon transmissions and repeatedly retransmits them to LUTs as the satellite orbits the Earth. This mode is possible only with 406 MHz beacons. It provides true global coverage.

---

[44] http://www.sarsat.noaa.gov/cospas_sarsat.html

The signals received by LEO satellites are relayed to a network of LUTs that locate the beacon by measuring the Doppler shift caused by the motion of the satellite with respect to the beacon. This process can locate beacons within an accuracy of 3.1 miles (5 km) for 406 MHz beacons. A low-power 121.5 MHz homing signal included in most 406 MHz beacons helps rescuers determine the final location as the search asset closes in on the beacon. The location data is then relayed to an MCC that alerts the appropriate RCC or an MCC in the appropriate country. If the alert is in an area covered by a foreign MCC, that MCC is alerted, and in turn, notifies its own RCC. The RCC then begins the actual search and rescue operation.

<u>Special note</u>

With the demise of the 121.5 signal processing, the aircraft still flying with the older ELTs have no satellite coverage. While it is standard practice for aircrews to monitor guard frequency (and required by some FARs) during oceanic crossings, and on Africa and polar routings, it is imperative that we always maintain listening watch unless you are radio limited. The 2010 price of a 406 MHz ELT is around $1000 plus installation. As of this writing the FAA and some other regulatory organizations around the world, have not mandated a compulsory date of change over. So, as we fly I hope everyone monitors 121.5 when possible. If you hear an ELT and report it to ATC, the controllers start a dialog with an RCC. After several 'hits' from various aircraft at different locations a triangulation position can be made.

AUSTRALIA SAR

Australia has a world renowned search and rescue service that spans the nation and covers 20 million square miles of the Indian, Pacific and Southern Oceans. The Rescue Coordination Center in Canberra is responsible for the national coordination of both maritime and aviation search and rescue. RCC Australia is also responsible for the management and operation of the Australian ground segment of the COSPAS-SARSAT distress beacon detection system. RCC Australia is staffed by search and rescue specialists who have a naval, merchant marine, air force, civil aviation or police service background. RCC Australia also coordinates medical evacuations, broadcasts maritime safety information and operates the Australian Ship Reporting System (AUSREP). [45]

INDIA SAR: The Indian Coast Guard is responsible for coordinating SAR operations in the Indian Maritime SRR. The Indian SRR is divided into four sub-regions, each with an assigned MRCC at Mumbai (Bombay), Chennai (Madras), Port Blair (Andaman & Nicobar Is) and MRSC at Porbandar. The MRCCs/MRSCs are co-located with the Coast Guard Regional Headquarters (RHQs) and co-ordinate missions with other agencies via a network of MRSCs. Merchant vessels plying through the Indian SRR may participate in a Computerised Vessel Reporting System for SAR known as "INDSAR". Position reporting by using two digit INMARSAT service code 43 via LES Arvi is voluntary and free of charge. Preferred inter RCC language is English.[46]

---

[45] http://www.amsa.gov.au/Search_and_rescue/

[46] http://www.indiancoastguard.nic.in/Indiancoastguard/sar/sar.html

NEW ZEALAND SAR

Major maritime, aviation and beacon-related search and rescue missions in New Zealand's search and rescue region are co-ordinated by Maritime New Zealand's Rescue Coordination Centre New Zealand (RCCNZ) located at Lower Hutt. Jointly, the RCCNZ and New Zealand Police can bring together over 100 rescue services and related agencies nationwide plus 10,000 search and rescue (SAR) personnel and volunteers.[47]

AFRICA SAR

The Aeronautical Subcommittee of Southern Africa is responsible for managing the efficient and effective provision of a search and rescue service in the aeronautical area of the southern countries. The aeronautical operations component of South Africa Search and Rescue is headed by the Chief of the search and rescue division. The Africa Rescue Coordination Center is located at Johannesburg International Airport and staffed by employees of the ATNS.

---

[47] NZ SAR Plan 2009-2014

RUSSIA SAR

The Search and Rescue Service of the Emergency Command (EMERCOM) of Russia includes seven regional Search and Rescue teams, consisting of 28 branches, and among them, eleven are engaged in search and rescue in water areas. The total EMERCOM research and rescue team staff has over 4000 personnel, with 1821 certified rescue workers.

UNITED KINGDOM SAR

The Maritime & Coastguard Agency (MCA) provides a response and co-ordination service for maritime SAR, counter pollution and salvage. The SAR role is undertaken by HM Coastguard, which is responsible for the initiation and co-ordination of civil maritime SAR. The Civil Aviation Division (CAD) has overall responsibility for UK civil aviation SAR and assigns appropriate SAR functions to the Ministry of Defense (MoD) and MCA. The MoD also establishes and maintains an Aeronautical Rescue Co-ordination Centre (ARCC) for the operation and co-ordination of civil and military aeronautical SAR.[48]

Her Majesty Coast Guard (HMCG) operates four SAR helicopter units providing suitably equipped helicopters and facilities at Sumburgh Airport (Shetland), Stornoway (Isle of Lewis), Portland and Lee-on-Solent. The helicopters provided have a full night/all weather capability (although some limitations exist with regard to freezing conditions) for civil maritime and civil aviation SAR and medical evacuation from ships and offshore installations.

[48] http://www.mcga.gov.uk/c4mca/mcga-uk_sar_framework_document.pdf

The current HMCG aircraft is the Sikorsky S61N. It has an endurance of approximately 4 hours. Allowing 30 minutes for winching up to 20 personnel on scene and retaining 30 minutes minimum landing fuel on completion of the task, the aircraft has a radius of action of around 180 NM. Range or time on scene can be extended by refueling at a forward base or on offshore platforms.

The RAF maintains one Nimrod MPA at 60 minutes readiness, 24 hours a day, at RAF Kinloss for SAR duties. The Nimrod can fly at high speed to a distance of approximately 800 nautical miles from base and then search for a period of 5 hours. Range can be extended at the expense of search time, or both may be extended by the use of in-flight refueling. The aircraft has a comprehensive suite of search sensors, most important of which is a radar optimised for over-water searches. A limited number of aircraft may also be fitted with an Infra Red (IR) capability. The Nimrod boasts a variety of communications equipment including UHF, VHF, HF and FM radios, and the combination of a powerful radar, long endurance and excellent communications, make the aircraft the platform of choice for directing activities at the scene. The aircraft itself can drop life rafts and survival equipment to persons in distress but is more frequently employed in vectoring ships and helicopters to the scene.

MoD maintains RAF Sea King helicopters at Boulmer, Chivenor, Leconfield, Lossiemouth, Valley and Wattisham which have a maximum endurance of 6 hours. This gives a radius of action of approximately 300 nautical miles from base. This can be extended by refuelling from forward bases, oil platforms or suitably equipped RN ships. All RAF SAR helicopters are equipped for full day/night all weather operations over land and sea (some limitations exist with regard to freezing conditions, but in general terms the helicopters are all weather capable) and have a full night vision goggle (NVG) capability. Crews are trained in NVG operations which, in itself, is a major enhancement to search capability. In addition, all RAF SAR helicopter rear crew are medically trained, with the winch man trained up to paramedic standard. Up to 18 persons can be carried, however, this is dependent on weather conditions and the distance of the incident from the helicopter's operating base. All RAF SAR helicopters are equipped with VHF (Marine and Air Band), UHF, HF and Mountain Rescue radios. They are also capable of homing to all international distress frequencies. The RN Sea Kings at Culdrose and Prestwick have an endurance of 5.5 hours, which gives a radius of action of approximately 250 nautical miles from base. These helicopters are held at similar readiness to the RAF SAR helicopters and are available for military and civilian tasking through the ARCC.

Below is a breakdown of the Non-US home bases for the long range aircraft (defined as able to reach out 750nm, and loiter/search for two hours. The list seems adequate, but if you study the locations while viewing a globe, you see large holes of non-coverage.

LOCATION ↓	ICAO	LAT/LONG (rounded)	OCEAN AREA SERVED ↓
LATIN AMERICA			

Guatemala City	MGGT	14° 35N 090° 32W	Equatorial Pacific, Caribbean
NORTH AMERICA WEST COAST			
Victoria, Canada	CYYJ	48° 39N 123° 26W	North Pacific
NORTH AMERICA EAST COAST			
Halifax, Canada	CYHZ	44° 53N 063° 31W	North Atlantic
ATLANTIC			
Reykjavik, Iceland	BIKR	65° 44N 019° 34W	North Atlantic, Barents Sea, McKinley Sea
Lajes Island, Portugal	LPPT	38 46N 009 08W	Atlantic
SOUTH AMERICA EAST COAST			
Zandery, Suriname	SMJP	05° 27N 055° 12W	Atlantic
Rio de Janiero, Brazil	SBGL	22 49S 043 15W	Atlantic
Buenos Aires, Argentina	SABE	34 34S 058 25W	Atlantic
Comodoro Rivadavia, Argentina	SAVC	45 47S 067 28W	Atlantic
Rio Gallegos, Argentina	SAWG	51 37S 069 19W	Atlantic + Pacific
Punta Arenas, Chile	SCCI	53 00S 070 51W	Atlantic + Pacific
SOUTH AMERICA WEST COAST			
Puerto Montt, Chile	SCTE	41 26S 073 06W	Pacific
Santiago, Chile	SCEL	33 24S 070 48W	Pacific
Antofagasta, Chile	SCFA	23 27S 070 27W	Pacific
Iquique, Chile	SCDA	20 32S 070 11W	Pacific
Isla Rey Jorge, Chile	SCRM	62 12S 059° 00W	Pacific
Isla De Pascua, Chile	SCIP	27 10S 109 25W	Pacific
AFRICA WEST COAST			
Sale, Morocco	GMME	34 03N	Atlantic

		006 45W	
Sal, Cape Verde	GVAC	16 45N 022 57W	Atlantic
Dakar, Senegal	GOOY	14 45N 017 29W	Atlantic
Douala, Cameroon	FKKD	04 01N 009 43E	Atlantic
Libreville, Gabon	FOOL	00 28N 009 25E	Atlantic
Luanda, Angola	FNLU	08 51S 013 14E	Atlantic
Cape Town, South Africa	FACT	33 59S 018 36E	Atlantic + Indian
AFRICA EAST COAST			
Mauritius Island, Rep of Mauritius	FIMP	20 26S 057 41E	Indian
MEDITERRANEAN			
Cairo, Egypt	HECA	30 07N 031 25E	Mediterranean
Tripolis, Libya	HLLM	32 54N 013 17E	Mediterranean
Akrotiri, Greece			Mediterranean 33 E
EUROPE WEST COAST			
Montijo, Portugal	LPMT	38 42N 009 02W	Atlantic
Lorient, France	LFRH	47 46N 003 26W	Atlantic
Kinloss, United Kingdom	EGQK	57 39N 003 34W	Atlantic + North Sea
Nordholz, Germany	ETMN	53 46N 008 40E	North Sea
WESTERN ASIA			
Muscat, Oman	OOMS	23 36N 058 17E	Indian
Karachi, Pakistan	OPKC	24 55N 067 10E	Indian
EASTERN ASIA			
Seletar, Singapore	WSSL	01 25N 103 52E	Indian + Pacific
Jakarta, Indonesia	WIII	06 07S 106 40E	Indian + Pacific
Surabaya, Indonesia	WARR	07 23S 112 47E	Indian + Pacific
Ujung Pandang, Indonesia	WAAA	05 03S 119 33E	Indian + Pacific
Ambon, Indonesia	WAPP	03 42S 125 05E	Indian + Pacific
Biak, Indonesia	WABB	01 12S	Indian + Pacific

		136 07E	
Guam, US	PGUM	13 29N 144 48E	Pacific
Wake Island, US	PWAK	19 17N 166 38E	Pacific
Kwajalein Island, Rep Marshall Isl	PKRO	09 24N 167 28E	Pacific
Honolulu, US	PHNL	21° 19N 157°55W	Pacific
AUSTRALIA WEST COAST			
Perth, Australia	YPPH	31 56S 115 58E	Indian + Southern
Learmonth, Australia	YPLM	22 14S 114 05E	Indian
Darwin, Australia	YPDN	12 24S 130 53E	Indian + Pacific 12 S
AUSTRALIA EAST COAST + NEW ZEALAND			
Adelaide, Australia	YPAD	34 56S 138 31E	Indian + Southern + Pacific
Melbourne, Australia	YMML	37 40S 144 51E	Indian + Southern + Pacific
Hobart, Australia	YMHB	42 50S 147 31E	Southern + Pacific
Sydney, Australia	YSSY	33 57S 151 11E	Southern + Pacific
Brisbane, Australia	YBBN	27 23S 153 07E	Pacific
Townsville, Australia	YBTL	19 15S 146 46E	Pacific
Port Moresby, Papua New Guinea	AYPY	09 27S 147 13E	Pacific
Lae, Papua New Guinea	AYNZ	06° 34S 146 44E	Pacific

What is missing from the above table are navy ships from many countries, maritime vessels in the fishing, tanker, container, freighter categories, and all sorts of commercial traffic overhead trying to find you.

I encourage everyone to spend some time thinking about what would happen if you are out on a crossing, and another aircraft ditches. How long could you stay on site…not everyone has fuel calculators or FMS computers? How could you expedite SAR as in do you have phone access direct to an RCC (see Chapter 17)? How would you interact with ATC if the NATs or PACOTs are heavily booked with traffic?

The World's Coast Guards use a variety of platforms to conduct its daily business. Cutters, medium boats and down to small boats are used on the water and fixed and rotary wing aircraft are used in the air.

Aircraft

There are a total of 211 aircraft in USCG inventory. Fixed-wing aircraft (C-130 Hercules turboprops and HU-25 Falcon jets) operate from large and small Air Stations. Rotary wing aircraft (H-65 Dolphin and HH-60 Jayhawk helicopters) operate from flight-deck equipped Cutters, Air Stations and Air Facilities.

Pictured is the HC-130J long range surveillance aircraft.

Pictured is the HH-65 Dolphin

Boats

All vessels under 65 feet in length are classified as boats and usually operate near shore and on inland waterways. Craft include: Motor Lifeboats, Motor Surf Boats, Large Utility Boats, Surf Rescue Boats, Port Security Boats, Aids to Navigation Boats, and a variety of smaller, non-standard boats including Rigid Inflatable Boats. Sizes range from 64 feet in length down to 12 feet.

Pictured is a 45′ medium response boat.

A "Cutter" is basically any CG vessel 65 feet in length or greater, having adequate accommodations for crew to live onboard. Larger cutters (over 179 feet in length) are under control of Area Commands (Atlantic Area or Pacific Area). Cutters at or under 175 feet in length come under control of District Commands. Cutters usually have a motor surf boat and/or a rigid hull inflatable boat onboard. Polar Class icebreakers also carry an Arctic Survey Boat (ASB) and Landing Craft. [49]

Pictured is the 418′ Coast Guard Cutter BERTHOLF.

[49] http://www.uscg.mil/datasheet/

MARITIME INTEGRATION TO SAR

Most aircrew members and aviation enthusiasts have visited the website www.flightaware.com. The website provides tracking of IFR flights which are airborne and reference data of individual tail numbers. Upon opening the website viewers see a US map with red dots for IFR traffic. On a typical day the site tracks 40,000+ IFR arrivals. Commercial flights and specific tail numbers can be searched for status and movements.

I bring up the Flight Aware website as it is very interesting to review, but I introduce it to relate to the maritime equivalent. There are several publicly accessible maritime web sites for SAR sources to reference for maritime assets. One is www.sailwx.info. The website is valuable to locate and communicate with a possible ocean-going resource for the SAR. Search and rescue centers worldwide use these types of sites.

Another very important marine tracking site is Automated Mutual-Assistance Vessel Rescue System (AMVER) to determine if an available ship is anywhere close to the downed aircraft. SAR centers obtain valuable data for referencing the maritime vessel. The centers can pull up and see much more data than the public website displays including classified data on naval asset locations.

An alternative site which gives additional ship tracking is www.marinetraffic.com/ais/. All three sites are invaluable to the RCCs around the world.

Here is a screen shot of a worldwide example of the sailwx site:

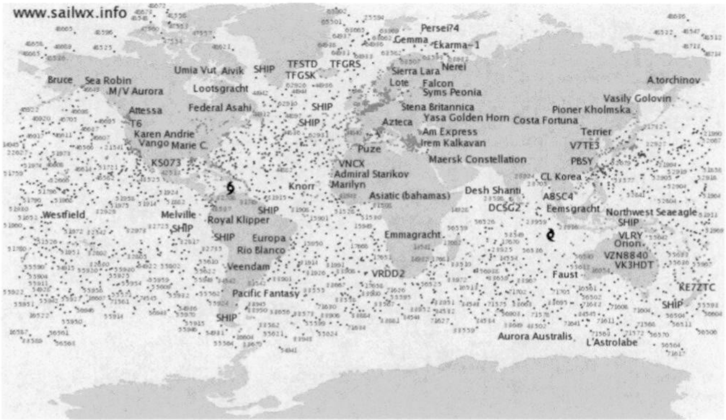

[50]

So, for instance, we can use an example of an aircraft coasting out of Anchorage for a Far East location. Suppose they pass 54 15°N and 166 30°W when they have an 'incident' and are forced to ditch. As they transmit distress messages and SAR kicks into gear, the rescue centers can view seaborne assets to determine if there is anyone close enough to dispatch toward the distressed aircraft. The web site can be zoomed in on to view the names of the ships in the area. The ship's name can be high-lighted and the details of the vessel can be viewed including type of ship, call sign, transponder codes, and all the communications frequencies and satellite phone numbers, and in some cases rescue equipment on the vessel. SAR centers can contact the ship's operating company and possibly the vessel's crew within minutes to relay data on the distressed aircraft.

Below is a screen shot centered on the Bering Sea to see what might be available for a rescue vessel.

---

[50] Courtesy Hal Mueller, publisher sailwx.info

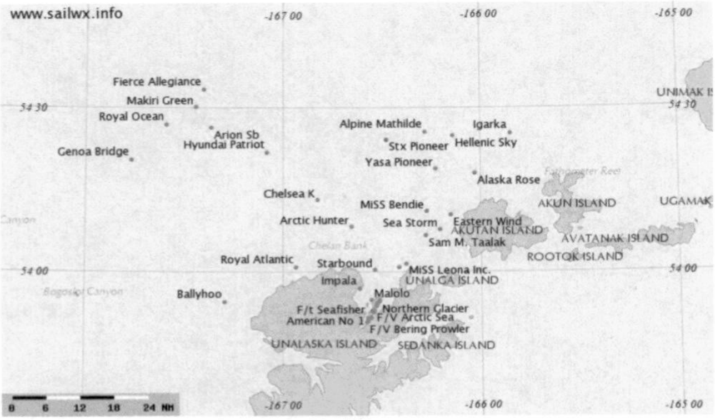

[51]

In this case, the closest ship with enough fuel to initiate search is the fishing boat Arctic Hunter, which is a 102 foot stern trawler fishing boat. The ship's normal movement speed is 12 to 14 knots. The ship is approximately 216 miles away and at 15 nautical miles per hour can reach the site in ~ 14 hours. It could be the first ship onsite. In the meantime, Coast Guard Air Station Kodiak would also launch multiple sorties of long-range aircraft with air droppable supplies.

So, spend some time thinking about the process of trying to board 300 people onto a fishing boat…in rough seas…at night…after they have been in rafts, or on the wing of the aircraft for 14 hours.

---

[51]Courtesy Hal Mueller, publisher sailwx.info

102 Foot Arctic Hunter Stern Trawler[52]

In the above screen shots, you will also notice multiple targets with serial type numbers. These targets are anchored buoys with transmitters. These buoys are dispersed worldwide and monitored for drift, temperature, and wave action. Some of these buoys are the components of the tsunami alert system known as Deep Ocean Assessment and Reporting of Tsunamis (DART). Some of them are combined with Tsunameters. Some of the buoys are for meteorological reporting only. Data from these buoys can be useful to determine the drift of a downed aircraft or disabled boat. In all cases, the buoys would be referenced and monitored for the continued triangulation of the rescue effort.

Below is a floating sea state and weather data gathering buoy which may or may not be combined with a Tsunameter.

52 Photo courteous of Jim Stone

Next is the more advanced full capability DART system buoy.

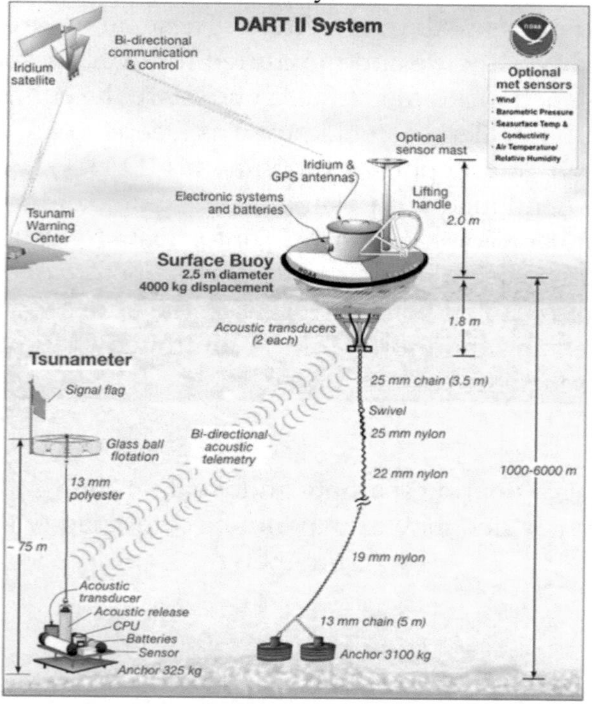

[53]

I have the pleasure of having an acquaintance who owns fishing boats. Big ones like you see on the program where several fishing boat crews are in competition off the Alaskan coast. They work in some of the harshest conditions of the sea. As we discussed how a pickup at sea would work, he remarked that he would rather be plucked out of the drink by a fishing boat that routinely maneuvers to pick up fishing gear, than a highly trained captain of a large commercial ship. It set us to thinking about how difficult it would be for that large ship to maneuver for the at-sea rescue.

[54]

So, just for another daydreaming drill, imagine you and possibly hundreds of your fellow passengers and crew standing on or floating next to the hull which was your airframe. And imagine you have been standing or floating

---

[53] http;//www.ndbc.noaa.gov/dart/dart.shtml

[54] Photo by author

for 72 hours. And from over the horizon comes something like The Maersk Denver. Imagine how difficult it would be for the captain and his crew to maneuver the ship like it is a canoe as he/she tries to pick up exhausted people. And if the seas are rough…well you get the picture.

For an even more complicated drill, imagine you and all passengers and crew stranded on floating polar pack ice after a successful ditching/ice landing. What type of extreme cold weather gear do we provide for passengers and what defensive devices do we carry for protection against polar bears? And consider how long it is going to take maritime resources to reach you…that is if they can reach you without an ice breaker ship leading the way. The FAA Cross Polar Working Group is thinking about it!

If you have ever wondered, large ocean crossing vessels usually have a crew of ~26. The men and women stand watch at their respective jobs in four-hour shifts.[55]

One of my training questions deals with how you would approach and be 'seen' by the personnel on the ship. There is a maritime regulation, 'International Regulations for Preventing Collisions at Sea' which were adopted as a Convention of the International Maritime Organization on 20 October 1972 and entered into force on 15 July 1977. This regulation states, "Every vessel must at all times keep a proper look-out by sight (day shape or lights by eyes or visual aids), hearing (sound signal or Marine VHF radio) and all available means (e.g. Radar, ARPA, AIS, GMDSS...) in order to make a full assessment of the situation and risk of collision."[56]

So, in theory there is always a human being on the bridge or assigned look-out station who is the guardian to prevent a collision while under way. So, in theory if you

---

[55] Interview John Howk; Jan 27, 2011

[56] http://www.admiraltylawguide.com/conven/collisions1972.html

fly your glider past the bridge of a vessel, someone 'should' see you and take appropriate action.

Since we pilots are occasionally pessimistic, the immediate question surfaces as, "Well, at 3am, what if the lookout on the bridge steps away for 90 seconds for a physiological need...?" It just was not your day.

ON THE WATER SURVIVAL

I do not pretend to be a survival expert or an instructor. But I have a compilation of 40+ years of training and offer some things to think about and problems to consider. Also included are advanced level words from professional rescue services.

With a floating fuselage, safety, survival and rescue are greatly increased when survivors remain near the airframe and/or the debris field. A floating fuselage and debris field have a much higher chance of being visually sighted by the rescuers, or on radar of a search aircraft. Even a fishing boat radar can spot an object as an aircraft tail at approximately three to five miles.

It is much easier to see debris or unusual items on the water. A historic example is the case in the rescue of the crewmembers of the USS Indianapolis in 1945. After the ship was torpedoed and sank, the men had been drifting in the water for five days. They were spotted by the pilot of a PV-1 Ventura Bomber on submarine watch, when he first noticed an oil slick and then "many men in the water". This is an excellent example of anything unusual on the water increasing the chance of being seen.

It is very important and worth expending effort to keep survivors together. Both physical value in having individuals to perform the myriad of needed tasks if the rescue takes longer than a few hours. There is also a very positive mental value in having the survivors together as the emotional stress is lessened if folks are not worrying about location and safety of family or co-travelers. It may seem trivial after a ditching, but reducing any stress among survivors is positive.

Concepts to think about as you build your ditching and survival plan.

- Communication via radios and SAT phones

- Signaling (flares, mirrors, dye). Remember DVDs and CDs make great signal mirrors with the sun and can be seen at great distance and altitude. Keep all devices 'at the ready', day and night which means sleeping in shifts.
- Dealing with first aid.
- Dealing with fatalities.
- Dealing with hypothermia.
- Raft management. Try to balance loads.
- Assignments to crew and able bodied passengers for:
    - bailing and raft maintenance
    - water production and allocation
    - food allocation
    - communications
    - signaling team
    - medical team
    - equipment gathering
    - spiritual leader
    - entertainment director

Open water survival depends on many factors. Water and air temperature, flotation devices, and drinking water to name a few. For those who make it out of the airframe, life rafts, seat cushions, and life vests will be invaluable. The crew who is trained in how to use the first aid kits, water kits, radios, and associated survival techniques should be distributed amongst the rafts and slides.

Following are words of John Isbell. John is a General Emergency Trainer. John is a retired US Coast Guard helicopter rescue swimmer and knows the business of survival inside and out. I was tempted to co-opt his words and re-write them to my style. And then I realized that his thoughts and feelings carry the weight of the professional he is. Here are his inputs to the chapter 'On the Water Survival'.

"When it comes to an aircraft going into the water, it can enter one of two ways; either uncontrolled or controlled. If it is an uncontrolled event, it is considered a crash. If it is a controlled event, it is a ditching. It is important to remember that since a ditching is a controlled event… it is survivable. What you do once you safely exit the aircraft will determine your fate.

Prior to ditching it is important to get a signal out and notify rescue resources. The Emergency Location Transmitter (ELT) is a signal on your aircraft that can be turned on one of three ways: manually, impact G-force, and water activation. Once the ELT is turned on it will send a signal via the 406 MHz frequency. The 406 MHz ELT is a much better frequency than the ELT's of the past due to the following factors: It has a GPS tracking that will get rescue resources within 2-3 square miles of the signal. It will display to the rescue resources the aircraft's tail number, size of aircraft, number of occupants the aircraft is capable of carrying, and most importantly, the owner and contact information needed to confirm if the aircraft is in distress or not. With the capabilities of being able to call an owner, or company, and with a much more accurate signal the response time and on scene time is drastically reduced with the 406 MHz ELT. Once all the occupants have exited the aircraft safely, the very first thing you must do is get out of the water if possible. The human body will lose body heat 25 times faster if in the water, than on land. If you are unable to get out of the water, then you must conserve as much energy as possible. The more energy you exert, the quicker you may become hypothermic. Regardless of the situation, the three areas that are important to protect are the head, armpits and groin. These three areas are where you will lose the majority of your body heat. If you have a life vest on, you can use the life vest to help keep your head out of the water, and then draw your legs to your chest to protect the groin, and tuck your arms in to protect the armpits.

Protection is the most important item a human needs in a survival situation. The second most important item is water, and the third most important item is food. If you are ever in a survival situation remember the rules of three: you can survive about 3 hours in a cold environment without protection, 3 days without water and 3 weeks without food. If a life raft is available, have occupants get into the raft, take a survivor count, and immediately get rid of all the sea water, close up the canopy and inflate the floor if it is cold outside. You want to create a barrier between you and the cold water and you will accomplish this by inflating the floor. It is important to keep yourself warm and dry, even in a life raft.

If at all possible, stay with the aircraft as long as it is safe to do so. Prior to deploying a life raft, it should be tied off to the inside of the aircraft. The best location to do this is to an attached seat belt. After the raft is tied off and inflated outside the other end of the inflation line will be attached to the raft… more than likely the boarding ladder. This line can be used by the survivors to pull them to the raft. If the aircraft starts to sink, the life raft is equipped with an automatic break away… so there is very little chance your raft will sink with the aircraft. The only time you should release yourself from an aircraft after a ditching is if the aircraft is sinking, there is a lot of debris in the area that could damage the raft, or if there is fuel surrounding the life raft. Other than those conditions always stay as close as possible to the aircraft. The aircraft is providing two types of signals: The electronic signal from the 406 ELT, and a visual target. Rescue resources will try to track down the signal and once they have found the aircraft they will determine their search route depending on the drift location of the debris. If you are still attached to the aircraft, this will make the search much easier for the rescue sources.

After everyone has safely boarded the life raft, the first thing that needs to be done is an accounting of all the survivors. After everyone has been accounted for the next step would be to elect a leader, or place someone in charge. Whoever is chosen should be someone with a positive attitude, not necessarily an individual with survival knowledge. The individual in charge will be responsible for maintaining order, keeping morale high, and providing everyone with a task to do to keep them focused on survival and getting rescued.

If a life raft is not available after a ditching, then everyone should get together in the huddle position. The huddle position is accomplishing many tasks: providing warmth and protection, providing support and morale, and providing a much larger target for the rescue resources. It is always important to stay together in any type of survival situation and even more so after a ditching. NEVER leave the group to look for help or supplies. IF someone must go looking for shelter, water, and/or food, do so but always go in a group of 2 or more individuals and remember how to get back.

Once rescue resources arrive on scene, more than likely a rescue swimmer, or diver, will enter the water to assist everyone into a rescue device. It is important to remember that if you are near the rescue device while it is being lowered to you, that you should let the device always touch the water first before grabbing hold. This includes the rescue swimmer as well. The device needs to be electrically grounded prior to touching so you don't risk getting shocked by the helicopter's static electricity.

If you are in a land survival situation, regardless of where you are, always take the life raft with you. The life raft is going to be your best item to use for protection. It is an instant tent, and will protect you from the heat, rain, snow, wind, etc. Not to mention all your survival items you will need for signaling will be located in the raft. When it comes to survival it is imperative that you always maintain a positive attitude. We must stay focused on the task at hand, and forget about the three D's… Death, Doom and Despair. As soon as negative thoughts enter the situation, it is very difficult to stay focused on survival and your situation could go downhill very fast."[57]

Following are more great survival words from other experts who know a lot about water survival. This information comes from the US Search and Rescue Task Force. [58]

<u>What To Do In The Water</u>

Cold water robs the body's heat much faster than cold air. If you should fall into the water, all efforts should be given to getting out of the water by the fastest means possible.

Physical exercise such as swimming causes the body to lose heat at a much faster rate than remaining still in the water. Blood is pumped to the extremities and quickly cooled. Few people can swim a mile in fifty degree water. Should you find yourself in cold water and are not able to get out, you will be faced with a critical choice - to adopt a defensive posture in the water to conserve heat and wait for rescue, or attempt to swim to safety.

Should you find yourself in the water, avoid panic. Air trapped in clothing can provide buoyancy as long as you remain still in the water. Swimming or treading water will greatly increase heat loss and can shorten survival time by more than 50%. The major body heat loss areas are the head, neck, armpits, chest and groin. If you are not alone,

[57] John Isbell, April 14, 2011, Savannah, Georgia

[58] http://www.ussartf.org/cold_water_survival.htm

huddle together or in a group facing each other to maintain body heat.

First Aid Considerations For Cold Water Victims

Treatment for hypothermia depends on the condition of the person. Mild hypothermia victims who show only symptoms of shivering and are capable of rational conversation may only require removal of wet clothes and replacement with dry clothes or blankets. In more severe cases where the victim is semi-conscious, immediate steps must be taken to begin the re-warming process. Get the person out of the water and into a warm environment. Remove the clothing only if it can be done with a minimum of movement of the victim's body. Do not massage the extremities. Lay the semi-conscious person face up, with the head slightly lowered, unless vomiting occurs. The head down position allows more blood to flow to the brain. If advanced rescue equipment is available it can be administered by those trained in its use. Warm humidified oxygen should be administered by face mask.

Immediately attempt to re-warm the victim's body core. If available, place the person in a bath of hot water at a temperature of 105 to 110 degrees. It is important that the victim's arms and legs be kept out of the water to prevent "after-drop". After-drop occurs when the cold blood from the limbs is forced back into the body resulting in further lowering of the core temperature. After-drop can be fatal. If a tub is not available, apply hot, wet towels or blankets to the victim's head, neck, chest, groin, and abdomen. Do not warm the arms or legs. If nothing else is available, a rescuer may use their own body heat to warm a hypothermia victim. Never give alcohol to a hypothermia victim.

Some Important Facts To Remember

Most persons recovered in cold water "near" drowning cases show the typical symptoms of death: Cyanotic (blue) skin coloration, no detectable breathing, no apparent pulse or heartbeat, and/or pupils fully dilated (opened). These symptoms, it was discovered, did not always mean the victim was dead. They were, on the other hand, the body's way of increasing its chances of survival through what scientists call the mammalian diving reflex. This reflex is most evident in marine mammals such as whales, seals or porpoises. In the diving reflex, blood is diverted away from the arms and legs to circulate (at the rate of only 6-8 beats per minute, in some cases) between the heart, brain and lungs. Marine mammals have developed this ability to the point where they can remain under water for extended periods of time (over 30 minutes in some species) without brain or body damage.

Humans experience the diving reflex, but it is not as pronounced as in other mammals. The factors which enhance the diving reflex in humans are:
Water temperature - less than 70 degrees or colder, the more profound the response and perhaps the more protective to the brain. Age - the younger the victim, the more active the reflex. Facial immersion - the pathways necessary for stimulating this series of responses seem to emanate from facial cold water stimulation. The diving reflex is a protective mechanism for humans in cold water immersions, but it may confuse the rescuer into thinking the victim is dead. Resuscitative efforts for these victims should be started immediately utilizing CPR in accordance with your training. Remember, numerous children have been brought up from freezing water after 30 minutes and been successfully resuscitated!

Expected Survival Time in Cold Water

Water Temperature	Exhaustion or Unconsciousness in	Expected Survival Time
70–80° F (21–27° C)	3–12 hours	3 hours – indefinitely
60–70° F (16–21° C)	2–7 hours	2–40 hours
50–60° F (10–16° C)	1–2 hours	1–6 hours
40–50° F (4–10° C)	30–60 minutes	1–3 hours
32.5–40° F (0–4° C)	15–30 minutes	30–90 minutes
<32° F (<0° C)	Under 15 minutes	Under 15–45 minutes

SEA STATE ANALYSIS

In oceanography, a sea state is the general condition of the free surface on a large body of water with respect to wind, waves, and swell at a certain location and moment. It is also characterized by statistics, including the wave height, period, and power spectrum.

The sea state varies with time, as the wind conditions or swell conditions change. The sea state can either be assessed by an experienced observer, like a trained mariner, or through instruments like weather buoys, wave radar or remote sensing satellites. The large number of variables involved in creating the sea state cannot be quickly and easily summarized, so simpler scales are used to give an approximate but concise description of conditions for reporting in a ship's log or similar record.

I throw this table into the book to continue working on your degree and to introduce a major factor that will contribute to a successful ditching. Understanding these numbers will also relate to the charts produced by Fleet Numerical Meterology Center.

Pierson Moskowitz Sea Spectrum[59]

Wind Speed (Kts)	Sea State	Significant Wave (Ft)	Significant Range of Periods (Sec)	Average Period (Sec)	Average Length of Waves (FT)
3	0	<.5	<.5 – 1	0.5	1.5
5	1	0.5	1 - 2.5	1.5	9.5
7	1	1	1 - 3.5	2	13
9	2	1.5	1.5 – 4	2.5	20
11	2.5	2.5	1.5 - 5.5	3	33
13	2.5	3	2 – 6	3.5	39.5
15	3	4	2 – 7	4	52.5
17	3.5	5	2.5 - 7.5	4.5	65.5
19	4	7	3 – 9	5	92
21	5	8	3 – 10	5.5	105
23	5	10	3.5 – 11	6	131.5
25	5	12	4 – 12	7	157.5
27	6	14	4 – 13	7.5	184
29	6	16	4.5 - 13.5	8	210
31	6	18	4.5 - 14.5	8.5	236.5
33	6	20	5 - 15.5	9	262.5
37	7	25	5.5 – 17	10	328.5
43	7	35	6.5 – 21	12	460
49	8	45	7.5 – 23	13	591

59 http://www.syqwestinc.com/support/Sea%20State%20Table.htm

DIRECT DIAL SEARCH AND RESCUE CENTERS

RCC	Area of SAR Coordination Responsibility	Phone Number[60]
Atlantic Coordinator	North Atlantic Ocean out to 40° west	+1 757 398-6700
Pacific Coordinator	Areas covered by RCC Seattle, Honolulu and Juneau.	+1 510 437-3700
RCC Miami	Caribbean Sea.	+1 305 415-6800
RCC Honolulu (operated as JRCC with DOD)	Hawaii, U.S. Pacific Islands and waters of Central Pacific Ocean	+1 808 535-3333
Sector Guam (under RCC Honolulu)	Western Pacific Ocean	+1 671 355-4824
RCC Juneau	North Pacific Ocean, Bering Sea, and Arctic Ocean	+1 907 463-2000
RCC Argentina	Buenos Aires Ushuaia	+54 1144 8024 86 +54 2901 4310 98
RCC Australia	Canberra	+61 262 306811
RCC Chili	Santiago Punta Arenas	+56 25305 941 +56 61202 161
RCC Fiji	Suva	+679 331 5380
RCC Mexico	Mazatlan	+52 669 985 3078
RCC New Zealand	Lower Hutt	+64 4577 8030

[60] All phone numbers validated March 2012

RCC South Africa	Cape Town	+27 2193 83300
RCC Tahiti	Papeete	+689 4624 32
RCC United Kingdom	Falmouth	+44 1326 317 575

61

61 http://www.uscg.mil/hq/cg5/cg534/RCC_numbers.asp

SUMMARY CHECKLIST OF PREPARATION

1. Have you chair-flown or hanger-flown engine failure to touchdown to iron out details of job duties?
2. Which way will you turn to get closer to rescue resources?
3. Is there an up-to-date and really well thought out ditching checklist for your aircraft?
4. Does YOUR ditching checklist have steps: 1) ELT - ON and 2) MODE C - 7700?
5. Who is running ditching checklist?
6. Who is in charge of engine re-start attempts?
7. Who is in charge of communication?
8. What is best glide configuration?
9. What is glide speed for various altitude blocks?
10. Are you going to seek help from any pilots in the back?
11. With engines failed, and no pressurization, do you need to make an emergency descent?
12. With engines failed, what electrical power will you have?
    - Radios
    - TCAS
    - Phone
    - Auto pilot
    - Navigation systems
13. With engines failed, how many minutes until landing?
14. If HMG or APU is started, or RAT activated, what will be powered?
15. Does your APU provide pressurization?
16. Do you have charts for sea state and surface winds?

17. Do you have a chart for local altimeter setting for night/IMC descent?
18. Do you have charts for basic ditching headings?
19. Can you contact SAR directly? Chapter 17 on page 139 has the phone numbers.
20. Are there any ships on the water in sight?
21. What configuration will you land with?
22. How will you put down flaps/ slats and how long will it take with reduced hydraulics and electrical power?
23. Minimum altitude to begin flap extension?
24. Will you use spoilers/ speed brakes for touchdown?
25. What will be reference speed for your approach and touchdown and do you have a system to compute speeds (without a runway for the box to look at)?
26. Pilot/ cockpit specific considerations:
    - Don oxygen masks?
    - Don smoke goggles?
    - Pillows to pad from yoke?
    - Outflow, cooling, and safety valves closed to enhance flotation?
    - Seat belts locked?
    - Seat position – back and down as much as possible?
    - Other pilots sent to passenger compartment to be the very best ABP in the most important locations?
    - Pre-position walk around bottles?
    - Everything in the cockpit tied down, stowed, or moved to back?

27. Airspeed. Airspeed. Airspeed. You must have a target speed in mind for touchdown. Work backwards from that speed to establish a reference speed for the last 1000 feet as you observe the immediate sea state to formulate what you want for the touchdown zone, and remember as you

encounter ground effect your touchdown aim point is going to extend. Too fast and you skip…to slow you stall. Chair-fly it.

28. Wings level. Wings level. Wings level. A wing tip in the water causes cartwheels. Bad. And if you have under wing engines, you must do everything possible to put the engines in the water at the same time. Think of the engines as 'speed brakes', but today they are 'water brakes'. Highly effective water brakes. Chair-fly this too.
29. Review the concept of rudder skid to maintain alignment with either trough or swell you decide to land on.

SEARCH AND RESCUE RADIO FREQUENCIES

HF FREQUENCIES FOR INTERNATIONAL DISTRESS
Aircraft HF radios transmit in the range 2.000 MHz to 29.999 MHz. There are no government agencies monitoring HF frequencies today.

AVIATION GUARD FREQUENCY
121.5

Aircraft out of radar range and over water also monitor 123.45 (fingers) to talk with other aircraft within radio range to exchange flight position, flight conditions, and important stuff like sports scores.
Aircraft VHF radios broadcast in the range 118.0 to 136.975 MHz.

MARITIME FREQUENCIES
Maritime radios operate on VHF as do aircraft. The maritime frequencies are in the 156.050 to 162.025 MHz range. For simplicity, marine radios use a channel system (like televisions at home) to associate with a frequency. Example, 'Channel 6' which broadcasts on 156.3 is for inter ship safety (the emergency channel) or 'Channel 12' which broadcasts on 156.6 is for port operations.

NOAA weather broadcasts seven weather channels as WX1 thru WX7 on 162.400 to 162.550MHz. Mariners turn their radios to the channel for the area they are in to listen to continuous broadcasts.

COAST GUARD FREQUENCIES

The Coast Guards around the world operate on multiple maritime channels and their corresponding frequencies.

SHIP TO SHORE FREQUENCIES

Also in the maritime channel lists, are set channels and their corresponding frequencies which can be used for basic telephone relays for non-emergency communications.

MILITARY MONITORS GUARD FREQUENCY

243.0

LORAN

The US COAST Guard shutdown all LORAN transmitters on February 8, 2010.

GPS now rules the world of navigation.

OUTSTANDING READING AND WATCHING

Perhaps the best website for researching survival and communications equipment: www.equipped.org

Movie: Castaway – watch the movie with an eye for ditching survival, you will see many new teaching points.

Captain Al Haynes discussion of the Sioux City crash landing.[62] One of the best readings of your aviation career.

Air France Flight 447 cockpit voice recorder with digital flight recorder[63] as aircraft control was lost over the South Atlantic

B-29 Ditching video March 9, 1945[64]

Lithium Battery Fire Test – FAA[65]

Adrift: 76 Days Lost At Sea
1982 story of a man sailing a sloop which capsizes and survives a month in a raft.

Our Last Chance
1989 Story of a couple whose sail boat is wrecked by pilot whales while 1200 miles west of Panama.

---

62 http://clear-prop.org/aviation/haynes.html

63 http://www.popularmechanics.com/technology/aviation/crashes/what-really-happened-aboard-air-france-447-6611877

64 http://www.youtube.com/watch?v=Cme9JcdSepA&feature=related

65 http://www.youtube.com/watch?v=gcd34tt8YPU

The Greatest Survival Stories Ever Told

Twenty seven stories of survival from the poles to the oceans.

The World's Most Amazing Survival Stories

Nineteen stories of survival from typhoon to crossing the Pacific on a raft.

Rough Water

Rescue at sea, solo around Antarctic, one man cruise thru the Roaring Forties.

SAMPLE SIMULATOR SCENARIOS

These scenarios are tailored for large aircraft but obviously can be tailored for any size operation.

Players required are SO - simulator operator. CAPT - captain, FO - first officer, LFA - lead flight attendant or purser, OAV - other aircraft in vicinity, ATC -air traffic controller, PM - phone monitor who also sends/responds to data messages.

SCENARIO #1 (QUICK DITCHING)

Aircraft at maximum cruise altitude at 50°N/ 30°W on an Atlantic crossing; or at 25°N/ 140°W on a Pacific crossing; or 80°N/ 40°W for a polar crossing; or 10°S/ 80°E for an Indian Ocean crossing. Day or night, IMC/VMC at operator's discretion.

ACTOR	ELAPSED TIME	ACTION
Simulator Operator	Start	Initiates cargo compartment fire
Simulator Operator	5	Cargo fire re-ignites
LFA	6	Calls cockpit to announce "smoke in cabin"
Simulator Operator	8	Initiates multiple smoke alarms
LFA	9	Calls cockpit to announce "heavy smoke and flames

		from under floor on left side
LFA	11	Calls cockpit to announce multiple pax overcome
	15	No response from rear of aircraft
Simulator Operator	16	Activates multiple sporadic electrical faults, fuel faults, hydraulic faults, fire faults

Crew Action Questions:

1. will captain leave cockpit to analyze/ fight fire
2. will captain send FO to analyze/ fight fire
3. How is crew coordination under pressure
4. ELT activation
5. Squawk 7700
6. when is decision to ditch made
7. to whom/ how does crew transmit distress signals
8. does crew prepare cockpit for water landing
9. is ditching checklist run
10. how was emergency descent handled

Ground Review:

1. ELT importance in non-radar environment discussion
2. Details of maximum descent profile
3. Importance of immediacy
4. Was first turn addressed
5. Were any ditching surface condition charts addressed
6. Any time for cockpit prep

SCENARIO #2 (DRIFTDOWN DITCHING)

Flight 123 at initial level off altitude, westbound passing 54°N/ 166°W after technical stop at Anchorage. Day or night, IMC/VMC at operator's discretion.

ACTOR	ELAPSED TIME	ACTION
LFA	2	Calls cockpit to see if captain wants beef or chicken.
ATC	4	"Flight 123 be advised we are receiving reports from USGS of Aviation Color Code Red volcano near Sedanka Island. Possibility of airborne contaminent is high. Sedanka is at your one o'clock, six miles."
Simulator Operator	5	Activate Elmo Fire. Activate compressor stalls.
PM	5	Data message from dispatch with details of aviation alert.
Simulator Operator	7	Activate fire warning on all engines.
LFA	7	Calls cockpit to advise heavy smoke in cabin
Simulator Operator	8	Activate engine seizure all engines.
OAV	8	"Anchorage this is N456. We have major problems lost engines. We are going down!"
Simulator Operator	9	Activate multiple smoke alarms.
Simulator Operator	10	Activate pressurization alarms (if no APU started)

Crew Action Questions:

1. Is pressurization addressed
2. How is crew coordination under pressure

3. Does crew communicate well with back end
4. ELT activation
5. Squawk 7700
6. when is decision to ditch made
7. to whom/ how does crew transmit distress signals
8. does crew prepare cockpit for water landing
9. is ditching checklist run

Ground Review:

1. What systems were powered
2. Was automation used
3. Was first turn addressed
4. ELT importance in non-radar environment discussion
5. Details of maximum descent profile
6. Importance of immediacy
7. Were any ditching surface condition charts used
8. Was consideration of cockpit prep made

AVIATION DEFINITIONS

ABP: Able bodied person; term used by flight attendants, loadmasters, and load technicians to identify a passenger who could help in an emergency.

ACARS: Aircraft communications addressing and reporting system.

ADS-B: Automatic Dependent Surveillance – Broadcast: Allows controllers to have much better 'view' of aircraft as to position and movement. The system can provide in the cockpit aural callouts for traffic conflicts and on the ground runway incursions.

AFIS: Automated Flight Information System: data transfer system for communicating between aircraft and ground support. Uses land based towers or satellites for communication. Similar to e-mail.

AIS: website depicting marine traffic.
www.marinetraffic.com/ais

AOR: Area Of Responsibility.

ARCC: Area Repeater Coordination Councils

ARPA: first version of the internet.

APU: Auxiliary Power Unit: typically a small jet engine onboard an aircraft to provide limited alternator/converter electrical power and some units can provide pressurized bleed air for engine start and pressurization (also while airborne)

BLUE WATER DITCHING: Any water encounter greater than five miles off a coastline. This could include open waters of the great lakes or any large body of water.

THE BOX: Slang term denoting the navigation system computers, flight management computers, or performance computers.

CB: Abbreviation for cumulonimbus thunderstorms. The worst of the worst which can contain severe up or down drafts, hail, lightning of multiple types, extreme winds.

COAST OUT: Aircraft departing land mass to continue flight overwater. A significant point as aircraft usually has an oceanic flight clearance prior to coast out. The crew also enters the mindset of being overwater and thus divert airfields becomes a much higher priority. Also known as "feet wet".

CHOPPING or SEGMENTING: Planning exercise to dissect a flight plan into segments and marking closest divert fields. The air fields are labeled with ICAO, or lat/long whichever you need for your FMS/UNS/GPS. Divert fields include engine out divert, loss of pressurization divert and medical emergency divert.

CIVIL AIR PATROL: Search and rescue organization in the United States which is 95% volunteers; organization provides inland and close in coastal search and rescue; organization is funded and managed by USAF; also provides counter drug services, fire spotting and community help services.

COASTAL WATER DITCHING: Any water encounter less than five miles off coast or on an inland water way.

CPDLC: Controller Pilot Data Link Capability (or communication).

CVR: Cockpit voice recorder.

DEAD STICK: Flying an aircraft (which is not a glider) with out power. As in it took off with engine power, but it is not going to land using engine power. This type of emergency flying/landing is much more complicated with today's aircraft which have hydraulically assisted flight controls, or may have 'fly-by-wire' controls meaning the controls in the cockpit produce an electrical signal which is transmitted over wire to the systems which are controlled by a motor apparatus.

DRIFT DOWN SPEED: Generally defined as the indicated airspeed in the cockpit which gives the aircraft the best range in event of an engine failure as it descends to a lower altitude.

EICAS: Engine indicating and crew alerting system. The system can be a tube type display or warning lights or round gages.

ELT: Emergency Locator Transmitter radio which broadcasts signals on frequency 121.5, 243.0 or 406 MHz. Activates either manually or upon crash or after water immersion.

EPIRB: Emergency Position Indicating Radio Beacon. Hand carried radio transmitter by backpackers, hikers, adventurers. Included in most life boat survival packs.

ETOPS: Extended Range Twin Engine Operations .

FDR: Flight data recorder.

FIRST TURN: Pointing the distressed aircraft in the direction of most suitable SAR base or toward the protected water such as leeside of an island.

FIXED WING: Typical aircraft with wings and fuselage.

FLOAT POSTURE: Attitude of the airframe at rest in the water. Think of it as nose up or nose down. This posture will be determined by fuel level in any tanks, load (weight of aircraft), and center of gravity of aircraft. The posture can also be heavily influenced by any damage to the hull. This posture will determine which exits or doors can be opened with the goal to allow no water to enter the fuselage. Everyone's goal must be to do everything possible to keep the fuselage afloat to enhance survival and greatly increase the probability of earliest rescue. A floating hull on the surface is astronomically easier to find versus a raft or people floating by themselves.

GMDSS: Global Marine Distress and Safety System. Radio operator training and certification to meet USCG requirements.

HF: High Frequency communications radio; in the range of 2.000 to 29.999 MHz range.

HMG: Hydraulic motor generator. Provides electrical power from a motor driven by aircraft hydraulic pressure.

ICAO: International Civil Aviation Organization; governing body for international aviation rules and regulations.

IFR: Instrument flight rules.

IMC: Instrument Meteorological Conditions.

JRCC: Joint Rescue Coordination Center. Military SAR combined with civilian SAR.

KIAS: Knots Indicated Air Speed. Airspeed indicated on instruments in cockpit. This speed is derived from air pressure as aircraft travels through the air measured from a tube on the outside of the aircraft.

KTAS: Knots True Air Speed. Indicated airspeed corrected for thin air encountered at high altitudes.

LUT: Local User Terminal. There are 45 computerized systems are located in 30 countries. The LUTs receive the signal from the satellites and forwards it on to the MCCs and then the RCCs which is responsible for SAR in that area

MCC: Mission Control Center. Normally operated by the government, military, coast guard, although a commercial company operates similar centers.

MOM: Slang term for your company or headquarters. Everyone has a MOM.

NATS: North Atlantic Tracks. assigned airways routings east or west bound across the northern section of the Atlantic Ocean. Daily routes are established based on velocity and size of the jet stream and temperatures at altitude. Routes are valid for a specific number of hours usually in the six to seven hour time period.

OACC: Oceanic Area Control Center.

PACOTS: Pacific Organized Track System. Established airways routings in the Pacific Ocean region.

PBE: Self contained personal breathing equipment. Think of this as a rubber or canvas or special plastic hood to put on over the head. The hoods generally have a small tank or generator to provide breathing air for the user. The hoods generally have air for 15 to 30 minutes.

POUR POINT: lowest temperature at which a liquid becomes semi-solid and loses its flow characteristics.

RAT: Ram Air Turbine. Small turbine driven by the air stream. It normally is contained in the wing or fuselage and is deployed (pops out into wind stream) after a total loss of electrical power. A RAT can drive hydraulic fluid which can in turn drive a generator, or a RAT can be a direct generator itself.

RHQ: Regional Headquarters.

RCC: Rescue Control Center.

ROTARY WING: aircraft with fuselage and spinning lifting blades (helicopter).

RVR: runway visual range. Measured by instruments and generally expressed in feet of visibility

SAR: Search and Rescue

SARR: Search and Rescue Repeater computer.

SARSAT: Search and Rescue Satellite System.

SEA STATE: Maritime term represented by a number from 0 to 9. The number indicates roughness of the sea with 0 meaning very smooth to 9 meaning very rough. See Section 7.

SRR: Search and Rescue Region which has geographic limits.

SOULS ONBOARD: Number which indicates live people on the airframe. Excludes counting cadavers which may be transported in baggage areas. Important for crash/rescue personnel to determine when all survivors are accounted for.

TCAS: Terminal Collision Avoidance System; onboard computer system which provides a display to the pilots of other airborne aircraft which could be a conflict.

UHF: Ultra high frequency; used by government/ military aircraft for air traffic control in the range of 225 to 400 MHz.

UNCONTAINED ENGINE FAILURE: Failure of an aircraft's engine characterized by parts or pieces which blast thru metal shrouds or engine cases. Engine manufacturers guard against this by lining the engine compartment with metal shields or kevlar type batting to keep any projectiles from escaping and doing damage to other parts of the airframe.

VHF: Very High Frequency radio; aviation radio range is 118.0 to 151.95 MHz.

VMC: Visual Meteorological Conditions.

VVI: Vertical Velocity Indicator which is measured in the cockpit as feet per minute. The instrument tells the pilots the rate of climb or descent.

GENERIC DITCH CHECKLIST

RUN IN CONJUNCTION WITH YOUR DITCHNG CHECKLIST

1. FLY THE AIRCRAFT
2. OXYGEN FOR CREW AND PAX
3. CHECKLIST FOR THE EMERGENCY AT HAND
4. ELT TO ON
5. SQUAK 7700
6. APU OR RAT OR HMG
7. REFERENCE ERGO BLUE TO ASCERTAIN LOCATION OF SHIPS BELOW YOU
8. ASSIGN RE-START DUTIES (CHECKLIST AND ACTIONS)
9. ASSIGN COMMUNICATION DUTIES (TELEPHONE TO SAR CENTER OR GIVE SAR NUMBER TO ANYONE WHO CAN CALL FOR YOU) AND TALK TO OTHER AIRCRAFT IN RADIO RANGE
10. ASSIGN DITCHING CHECKLIST DUTY
11. DETERMINE FIRST TURN
12. AUTOMATE GLIDE (AUTOPILOT OR TRIM FOR AIRSPEED)
13. ANNOUNCE TO CABIN
14. ANNOUNCE TO WORLD
15. ANY OTHER PILOTS ON-BOARD
16. ESTABLISH LOOKOUT FOR ANY SHIPS ON WATER – GIVE THIS DUTY TO ALL <u>CREW AND PAX!</u>
17. OXYGEN MASK
18. GOGGLES
19. COATS OR PILLOWS FOR PADDING
20. ALL OUTFLOW VALVES CLOSED
21. SEAT DOWN, BACK AND LOCKED
22. ANNOUNCE ON GUARD FINAL LAT/LONG AND HEADING AT 2000 AGL

ACKNOWLEDGEMENTS

I can never say Thank You enough to the big hearted and gracious friends, co-workers, industry experts, pilots in command, instructor pilots, standards pilots, test pilots, international captains, photographers, ideas people, FAA representatives, military, NOAA, and coast guard friends, and most of all Diana my wife who has endured the efforts of my passion for years.

Jim Stabile. CEO Aerodynamic Systems. Inventor of application ERGO BLUE.

Betsy Barajas, Alaska Airlines.

Lt Colonel Dwane R. Boucher, USAFR (ret). Retired Continental Airline.

Ana Prieto-Curtis, executive assistant, Flight Safety International.

Louisa Fisher, emergency trainer, Flight Safety International.

John Gowey, Chief Pilot, Kenmore Air, Seattle, WA.

Ian Gregor, FAA Communication Manager, Western- Pacific Region.

Jeff Griffin, US Coast Guard (RET), District 13 Headquarters, Seattle, WA.

Brad Kidwell, Techno-Sciences, Beltsville, MD.

Major Lee (Ice) Icenhour, US Air Force (RET). Currently flying Gulfstreams.

John Isbell, helicopter rescue swimmer, US Coast Guard (RET).

Marty Mauney, Boeing Aircraft Company, Seattle, WA (RET), advisor, friend.

Don Myers, US Coast Guard (RET). Retired Delta. Advisor, friend, co-worker.

Major Wade Morton, US Air Force (RET). Advisor, friend. Currently at Jeppsen, Denver, CO.

Captain Salvatore Palmeri, US Coast Guard, Group Commander USCG Group/Air Station Humbolt Bay.

Lt Colonel Tony (Marlboro) Piso, US Air Force (RET), advisor, friend. Currently flying Bombardier C-350 at NetJets.

Commander Rob Poston, National Oceanic Atmospheric Administration (Pilot/ Commissioned Officer RET). Editor, advisor, friend, co-worker. Currently at NetJets.

Amy Sexton, AG1, US Navy, NAF Comp Whidbey Island, WA.

Joe Sherman, US Coast Guard (RET).

Major Michael Stevens, US Air Force Reserve, C-17 pilot. Currently flying Gulfstreams. Advisor, friend.

Jim Stone, President Alaska Bering Sea Crabbers, advisor, friend.

Dave Strelinger, Instructor Pilot Alaska Airlines.

NOTES